The Microwave Convection Oven Cookbook

Contents

PRECAUTIONS TO AVOID POSSIBLE EXPOSURE TO EXCESSIVE MICROWAVE ENERGY

(a) **Do not attempt to operate this oven with the door open** since open-door operation can result in harmful exposure to microwave energy. It is important not to defect or tamper with the safety interlocks.

(b) **Do not place any object** between the oven front face and the door or allow soil or cleaner residue to adccumulate on sealing surfaces.

(c) **Do not operate the oven** if it is damaged. It is particularly important that the oven door close properly and that there is no damage to the:
    (1) Door (bent)
    (2) hinges and latches (broken or loosened)
    (3) door seals and sealing surfaces

(d) **The oven should not be adjusted or repaired** iby anyone except perperly qualified service personnel.

◀ *Chicken A La Roma;*
for recipe, see p. 51

Introduction

Microwave

In microwave ovens, household electricity is converted into a type of high frequency radiowave by a magnetron tube. These microwaves cause the water molecules within the food to vibrate at extremely high speeds. This friction produces the intense heat which cooks the food.

Foods cooked in the microwave oven are placed directly on the turntable.

One advantage of microwave cooking is that food can be heated directly in the serving utensil. Not all serving utensils are microwave oven safe. Check manufacturer's recommendation before using.

Convection

As in a conventional oven, the convection oven has a heating element necessary to produce crisp, brown exteriors. However, in a convection oven a fan is used to circulate the hot air which results in more uniform cooking.

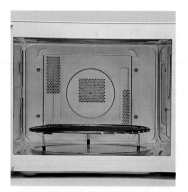

The metal accessory rack is placed directly on oven turntable during all convection cooking.

When baking cookies in this oven, the best results are obtained by using the convection setting. The circulation of hot air during convection cooking gives cookies crisp, brown exteriors along with chewy interiors.

Combination

During combination cooking, the oven automatically alternates between convection and microwave heating. Combination cooking gives the advantage of convection browning and the speed of microwaving.

Combination cooking is ideal for roasting meat. The circulating hot air quickly browns the meat and seals in the juices.

When cooking by combination, casseroles require less time than when conventionally cooked and less attention than when microwaved.

Utensil

The type of utensil used will depend upon the cooking method selected. Although there is cookware on the market specifically designed for use in combination ovens, there is no need to purchase new utensils. Always check the manufacturer's recommendation before use.

Paper, glass and microwave-safe plastic utensils are ideal for use in microwave ovens.

To make sure a dish is microwave safe, place it in the oven with 1 cup water in a glass measure. Microwave at HIGH (10) 1 minute. If dish remains cool, it is suitable for microwaving.

This oven comes equipped with a metal accessory rack. Consult charts and recipes for recommended use of accessories.

Utensils which are normally used in a conventional oven can also be used when convection cooking.

Combination cookware must be heat resistant up to 400°F. Oven-safe glassware and ceramic dishes are ideal for combination cooking.

Cookware and Utensil Guide

TIPS: **1.** Always check the manufacturer's recommendation before using any utensils in the oven.
2. Make certain that the utensil will fit on the oven turntable or shelf.

Type of Utensil	Microwave	Convection	Combination
Aluminum Foil	For Shielding	Yes	For Shielding
Browning Dish	Yes	No	No
Brown Paper Bags	No	No	No
Dinnerware			
Oven/Microwave Safe	Yes	Yes	Yes
Non Oven/Microwave Safe	Yes	No	No
Disposable Polyester			
Paperboard Dishes	Yes	Yes* heat resistant up to 400°F	Yes* heat resistant up to 400°F
Glassware			
Oven Glassware & Ceramic	Yes	Yes	Yes
Non Heat Resistant	No	No	No
Metal Accessory Racks	No	Yes	Yes
Metal Cookware	No	Yes	No
Metal Twist-Ties	No	Yes	No
Oven Cooking Bag*	Yes	Yes	Yes
Paper Towels and Napkins	Yes**	No	No
Plastic Dishes			
Microwave Safe	Yes	Yes* heat resistant up to 400°F	Yes* heat resistant up to 400°F
Plastic Wrap	Yes	No	No
Straw, Wicker, Wood	Yes	No	No
Thermometers			
Microwave Safe	Yes	No	No
Conventional	No	Yes	No
Wax Paper	Yes	No	No

* Always check manufacturer's recommendation.

** Do not use paper towels which contain synthetic fiber such as nylon woven into them. Synthetic fibers may cause the towel to ignite.

Microwave Techniques

The characteristics of food and the application of certain techniques will influence the speed and effectiveness of microwave cooking. While the techniques may be familiar, the way they are used may be somewhat different because of the unique way in which microwave energy cooks.

STARTING TEMPERATURE Suggested cook times in this book are based on normal storage temperatures. Foods which are refrigerated or frozen may require longer cooking times than foods stored at room temperature.

DENSITY In both conventional and microwave cooking, dense foods, such as potatoes, take longer to cook or reheat than light porous foods such as a piece of cake, bread or a roll.

MOISTURE CONTENT Moisture of food affects how it cooks. Very moist foods cook evenly because microwave energy is attracted to water molecules. Food with low moisture content should be covered during cooking and allowed to stand after cooking so that heat can disperse evenly.

QUANTITY In microwave cooking, where time is directly related to the number of servings, small amounts of food take less time to cook than large ones.

SIZE Foods which are similar in size and shape cook more evenly. Small pieces cook faster than large ones. When cooking large pieces of food such as a roast, the power level may be reduced to allow for more even cooking.

STIRRING For best results, some foods may need to be stirred from the outside to the center once or twice during cooking. Foods which require constant stirring conventionally will need only occasional stirring. When possible, stir foods before serving.

ROTATING Repositioning a dish in the oven during cooking is unnecessary in models featuring a turntable.

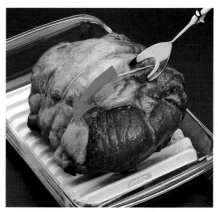

TURNING OVER When microwaving some foods, such as roasts or frozen meat patties, it may be necessary to turn food over after half of cooking time for best results.

STAND TIME In microwaving, stand time is necessary to allow foods to finish cooking. For example, during stand time, moist surface areas on cakes will disappear and the internal temperature of a roast will continue to rise.

TEMPERATURE Foods with delicate textures are best cooked at lower power levels. Using the temperature probe can prevent milk-based liquids from over cooking. To ensure thorough heating, foods should reach a temperature of 160°F to 165°F before serving.

DO NOT MICROWAVE. Do not cook eggs in shells. Avoid heating foods in narrow necked jars and bottles. Always remove lids from wide necked jars before warming food. Heating baby food in jars is not recommended.

Microwave Techniques

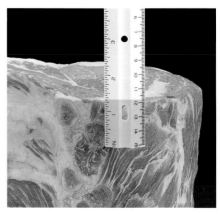

Microwaves pass through paper, glass, plastic and ceramic utensils. These materials are ideal for microwave oven cooking because they allow microwave energy to penetrate the food. Paper towels and napkins absorb moisture in foods such as bacon and aid in retaining moisture in foods such as breads and rolls.

Microwaves are reflected by metal. Foil wrapped boxes, aluminum containers deeper than ¾ inch, metal baking utensils and conventional meat thermometers are not suitable for use in microwave ovens. Do not use glass, pottery or pyroceram utensils with metal trim or fittings.

Microwaves penetrate to a depth of about ¾ to 1¼ inches. This microwave energy causes molecules within the food to vibrate, producing the heat necessary to cook the food.

Foods should be arranged with the meatiest portions around the outer edge of the dish and thinner pieces toward the middle. This enables thick portions to cook completely without overcooking thin pieces.

Size and shape of a container will influence the microwave cooking time. A shallow casserole exposes more food surface to microwave energy and will require less time to cook than taller utensils holding the same amount. Since microwaves penetrate from all sides, round shapes and rings cook more evenly.

Many convenience foods are packaged in containers designed especially for use in microwave ovens. Consult package instructions for cooking procedures.

PRICK FOODS TO RELEASE PRESSURE. Steam causes pressure to build in foods which are tightly covered by a skin or membrane. Prick potatoes, egg yolks and chicken livers to prevent bursting.

ARRANGEMENT Place individual items, such as custard cups or baked potatoes in a ring. Allow space between foods so that energy can penetrate from all sides.

SHIELDING When microwave cooking or defrosting, foods may be shielded to prevent overcooking. Use small strips of foil to shield thin parts, such as the tips of wings and legs on poultry, which may cook before larger parts.

SHAPE OF FOOD When microwaving, arrange foods with the thickest or less tender portions to the outside of the dish. This prevents thinner more tender pieces from overcooking. Arrange foods of equal size in a ring, leaving the center empty.

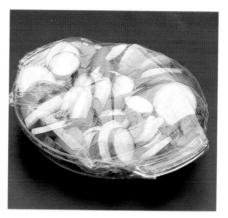

COVERING To cook quickly and retain moisture, cover dish with a lid or plastic wrap. Vent plastic wrap by turning back one edge or corner so that excess steam can escape. To hold in heat and prevent spatters without steaming, use wax paper.

POROUS COVERS Paper towels or napkins allow steam to escape, absorb moisture and prevent spattering.

Defrosting Techniques

See Pages 130-131 For Defrosting Chart.

Casseroles, soups and stews will require stirring once or twice during defrosting.

Remove meat from the original wrapper and place in baking dish. After first half of defrosting time, break up or separate ground beef, steaks, chops, chicken pieces or fish fillets. Remove defrosted areas and return remainder to oven to complete defrosting.

Turn large roasts, whole chickens and Cornish hens over after half of defrosting time. Shield warm areas with small pieces of foil. For whole poultry, start with the breast side down. Defrost meats and poultry only until the surface feels cool but not icy.

Power Level Chart

Power Level		Percent of Power
HIGH	(10)	100%
	(9)	90%
	(8)	80%
MEDIUM HIGH	(7)	70%
	(6)	60%
MEDIUM	(5)	50%
	(4)	40%
LOW/DEFROST	(3)	30%
	(2)	20%
WARM	(1)	10%

Delicate foods such as cheesecake, frosted cakes or cream pies should be removed from original wrapper and placed on a serving plate. Microwave at LOW (3) until a wooden pick can be inserted in the center easily. Let cakes and pies stand 15 to 25 minutes before serving.

Microwave Adapting

When adapting recipes for the microwave, it is best to start with a familiar recipe. Knowing how the food should look and taste will help when adapting it for microwaving. Foods that require browning or crisp, dry surfaces will cook best when using the convection or combination setting.

- Refer to similar microwave recipes for cooking techniques, power levels and microwaving time.

- Moist foods such as vegetables, fruits, poultry and seafood microwave well.

- Rich foods such as bar cookies, moist cakes and candies are suitable for microwaving because of their high fat and sugar content.

- Reduce conventional cooking time by one-third to one-half. Check food after minimum time to avoid overcooking.

- Small amounts of butter or oil can be used for flavoring but are not needed to prevent sticking.

- Seasonings may need to be reduced. Salt meats and vegetables after cooking.

- Liquids may need to be reduced.

Recipe Conversion

Conventional Spanish Rice

1 lb. ground beef
1½ cups water
¾ cup long grain rice
2 tablespoons chili powder
2 tablespoons instant minced onion
½ teaspoon salt
⅛ teaspoon pepper
1 (28 oz.) can whole tomatoes, cut up

In 10-inch skillet, crumble ground beef. Cook, uncovered, over medium-high heat 10 minutes; drain. Add water, rice, chili powder, onion, salt, pepper and tomatoes. Mix well. Cover and cook over medium heat 35 to 40 minutes.

Total Cooking Time 45 to 50 Minutes
Serves 4 to 6

Microwave Spanish Rice

1 lb. ground chuck
1 cup uncooked instant rice
2 tablespoons chili powder
1 tablespoon instant minced onion
½ teaspoon salt
⅛ teaspoon pepper
1 (28 oz.) can whole tomatoes, cut up

In 2-quart casserole, crumble beef. Cover and microwave at HIGH (10) 6 to 8 minutes until no pink remains; drain. Add instant rice, chili powder, minced onion, salt, pepper and tomatoes. Mix well. Cover. Microwave at HIGH (10) 12 to 14 minutes, stirring after 6 minutes. Stir before serving.

Total Cooking Time 18 to 22 Minutes
Serves 4 to 6

CONVENTIONAL

MICROWAVE

Introduction

Convection Cooking

In a convection oven, a fan circulates hot air around the food and evenly distributes it throughout the oven cavity. The circulating air uniformly heats the food producing a crisp, brown exterior. In most cases, convection baking and roasting temperatures will be the same as those recommended for conventional cooking. Refer to individual charts and recipes for best baking temperatures.

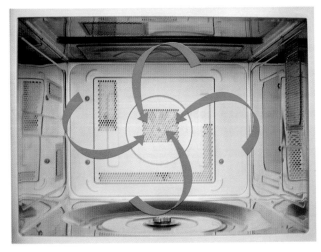

Circulating air prevents heat from collecting at the top of the oven and creates a more uniform oven temperature.

Convection Techniques

Many of the techniques used in conventional cooking are also important when cooking by convection. Following these recommendations will assure exceptional baking results.

The same cookware and utensils that are normally used when conventionally baking can also be used in convection ovens. For best results, however, use shiny, aluminum utensils.

Dark or matte finish utensils will produce darker browning on food surfaces.

Heat-resistant paper and plastic containers that manufacturers recommend for use in conventional ovens can be used in convection ovens. Plastic cooking utensils that are heat resistant to temperatures of 400°F are also suitable.

Use a pan with low sides whenever possible. A shallow pan allows air to circulate around the food more efficiently.

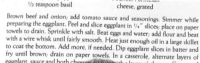

As a general rule, convection baking temperatures will be the same as those used in a conventional oven.

Remember, oven walls, shelves and cooking utensils do get hot during convection cooking. Always use dry oven mitts when removing utensils from the oven.

Combination

Combination cooking combines the best features of convection and microwave. Foods cook quickly with less manipulation than when microwaved and achieve the crisp, brown exterior of convection cooking. When combination cooking, reduce conventional cooking times by one-fourth to one-third. Always check for doneness at minimum time.

Glass baking dishes, stoneware and pottery utensils designed for use in both conventional and microwave ovens, may be used for combination cooking.

Convenience foods packaged in heat-resistant paper and plastic containers that are recommended for use in conventional ovens can be used when combination cooking. Plastic cooking utensils that are heat resistant to a temperature of 400°F are also suitable.

When checking foods for doneness in the combination oven, use conventional techniques. For example, cake is done when a toothpick inserted in the center comes out clean. The top will also appear dry and spring back when touched lightly.

Aluminum cake pans and utensils are not recommended for use in combination cooking. Paper products and plastic utensils, recommended for microwave use only, cannot be used in combination cooking. Always check the manufacturer's recommendations.

Convection Results

Any food that can be cooked in a conventional oven cooks beautifully in a convection oven. In fact, professional chefs choose convection ovens for consistently superior baking and roasting results.

Convection roasting is ideal for meats. Moisture and flavor are sealed in quickly as circulating hot air browns the surface.

Chicken and other poultry develop crisp golden skin but stay juicy and tender.

Casseroles may bake in less time or at a lower temperature than in a conventional oven.

Pies baked in a convection oven are evenly browned, tender and flaky.

The convection oven's uniform temperature helps keep airy foods, such as cream puffs, high and light.

Breads baked in the convection oven have consistent texture and evenly browned crusts.

Appetizers & Beverages

Garlic Shrimp

2 tablespoons butter
2 cloves garlic, minced
¼ lb. fresh medium shrimp, peeled and deveined
1½ teaspoons fresh parsley, snipped
1½ teaspoons grated Parmesan cheese

In small mixing bowl, combine butter and garlic. Microwave at HIGH (10) 1 to 2 minutes. Add shrimp and parsley. Microwave at MEDIUM HIGH (7) 2 to 3 minutes; stir after 1 minute. Stir in Parmesan cheese.

Total Microwave Cooking Time 3 to 5 Minutes
Makes 4 appetizer servings

Oriental Meatballs

1 lb. ground beef
1 lb. ground pork
½ cup canned water chestnuts, drained, finely chopped
¼ cup green pepper, finely chopped
3 green onions, chopped
2 tablespoons soy sauce
2 tablespoons pineapple juice
Sauce:
1 (20 oz.) can chunk pineapple
1 tablespoon instant beef bouillon granules
¼ cup brown sugar, packed
2 tablespoons cornstarch
2 tablespoons vinegar
⅔ cup water

Drain pineapple, reserving liquid. In large mixing bowl, combine beef, pork, water chestnuts, green pepper, onions, soy sauce and 2 tablespoons pineapple juice; mix well. Shape into 1-inch meatballs. Arrange in 2-quart oblong glass baking dish. Cover with plastic wrap, turning back one corner to vent. Microwave at HIGH (10) 8 to 10 minutes until thoroughly cooked. Drain and set aside.

In 4-cup glass measure, combine remaining pineapple juice, beef bouillon, brown sugar, cornstarch, vinegar and water. Microwave at HIGH (10) 3 to 4 minutes until mixture thickens; stir after 2 minutes. Add pineapple. Pour sauce over meatballs. Microwave at HIGH (10) 2 to 3 minutes until heated through.

Total Microwave Cooking Time 13 to 17 Minutes
Makes about 32 meatballs

Cheese Ball

¼ cup butter
1 (3 oz.) pkg. cream cheese
1 teaspoon Worcestershire sauce
½ teaspoon onion powder
⅛ teaspoon garlic powder
3 cups Cheddar cheese, shredded
½ cup walnuts, finely chopped or fresh parsley, snipped
Assorted crackers

Place butter in 1-cup glass measure. Microwave at HIGH (10) 15 to 20 seconds until butter softens. Place cream cheese in 2-quart glass mixing bowl. Microwave at MEDIUM (5) 30 to 40 seconds until cream cheese softens. Blend in softened butter, Worcestershire sauce, onion powder, garlic powder and Cheddar cheese. Beat at medium speed of electric mixer until smooth. Shape into a 4-inch ball. Roll in nuts or parsley to coat. Refrigerate for 3 hours. Serve with crackers.

Total Microwave Cooking Time ¾ to 1 Minute
Makes one 4-inch cheese ball

Appetizers & Beverages

▲ *Vegetable Crispers, Spicy Chicken Wings and Cocktail Reubens*

Place buttered vegetables into plastic bag with crumb mixture and shake to coat evenly.

Vegetable Crispers

½ cup dry bread crumbs
½ cup grated Parmesan
  cheese
1 teaspoon tarragon leaves,
  crushed
1 teaspoon paprika
Dash pepper
1 cup broccoli flowerets
1 cup cauliflower flowerets
1 medium zucchini, sliced
  ½-inch thick
12 small whole mushrooms
½ cup butter, melted

Combine bread crumbs, Parmesan cheese, tarragon, paprika and pepper in plastic bag. Taking several pieces at a time, dip broccoli, cauliflower, zucchini and mushrooms into melted butter. Place into plastic bag with crumb mixture and shake to coat evenly. Repeat until all vegetables are coated. Arrange in single layer in 2-quart oblong glass baking dish. Place metal accessory rack on turntable. Preheat oven to 350°F. Convection Bake 15 to 18 minutes until lightly browned.

Total Convection Cooking Time 15 to 18 Minutes
Makes about 40 appetizers

Cocktail Reubens

36 slices cocktail rye bread,
  toasted
½ cup Thousand Island
  dressing
1 (8 oz.) can sauerkraut,
  rinsed and drained
¼ lb. thinly-sliced corned
  beef
1 (6 oz.) pkg. Swiss cheese
  slices, each slice cut into
  4 squares

Arrange half of bread slices on a 12-inch pizza pan. Spread each slice with about ¾ teaspoon Thousand Island dressing. Add small amount of sauerkraut and corned beef to each slice. Top each with 1 square Swiss cheese. Place metal accessory rack on turntable. Preheat oven to 375°F. Convection Bake 5 to 8 minutes until cheese melts and edges are lightly browned. Repeat with remaining bread slices.

Total Convection Cooking Time 5 to 8 Minutes
Makes 36 appetizers

Spicy Chicken Wings

½ cup sour cream
2 tablespoons red onion,
  finely chopped
1 clove garlic, crushed
¼ cup fresh parsley, minced
1 cup mayonnaise
¼ cup blue cheese,
  crumbled
1 tablespoon lemon juice
¼ teaspoon seasoned salt
¼ teaspoon freshly ground
  black pepper
⅛ teaspoon cayenne pepper
¼ cup butter, melted
1 teaspoon hot sauce
12 chicken wings, separated
  into 2 pieces

In small mixing bowl, combine sour cream, onion, garlic, parsley, mayonnaise, blue cheese, lemon juice, seasoned salt, pepper and cayenne pepper. Mix well and refrigerate.

Place metal accessory rack on turntable. Preheat oven to 450°F. In small mixing bowl, combine melted butter and hot sauce. Place chicken wings on 12-inch pizza pan. Brush wings with butter mixture. Convection Bake 30 to 35 minutes until golden brown. Serve with refrigerated dip.

Total Convection Cooking Time 30 to 35 Minutes
Makes 5 to 6 appetizer servings

Appetizers & Beverages

▲ *Sausage Muffin Teasers and Tiny Chicken Turnovers*

Sausage Muffin Teasers

½ lb. hot bulk pork sausage
2 cups all-purpose flour
1 tablespoon baking
    powder
1 tablespoon sugar
¼ teaspoon salt
⅛ teaspoon thyme
Dash cayenne pepper
1 cup milk
1 egg, slightly beaten
¼ cup vegetable oil
½ cup extra sharp Cheddar
    cheese, shredded
2 tablespoons onion, finely
    chopped

In 1-quart casserole, place sausage; cover. Microwave at HIGH (10) 3 to 5 minutes until browned, stirring to crumble after 2 minutes. Drain well; set aside. In medium bowl, combine flour, baking powder, sugar, salt, thyme and cayenne pepper; make a well in center of mixture. Combine milk, egg and oil. Add to dry ingredients, stirring just until moistened. Stir in sausage, cheese and onion.

Place metal accessory rack on turntable. Preheat oven to 425°F. Spoon batter into greased 1¾ x 1-inch muffin pans, filling three-fourths full. Convection Bake 13 to 17 minutes. Remove from pans immediately.

Total Convection Cooking Time 13 to 17 Minutes
Makes about 4 dozen muffins

Barbecue Baby Back Ribs

2 lbs. baby back ribs, cut in
    serving size pieces
2 cups hot tap water
1 (18 oz.) bottle barbecue
    sauce

In 2-quart casserole, place ribs and water. Cover. Microwave at MEDIUM (5) 60 to 65 minutes, rearranging after 40 minutes. Drain well. Pour barbecue sauce over ribs. Cover. Microwave at HIGH (10) 5 to 7 minutes until heated through.

Total Microwave Cooking Time 1 Hour 5 Minutes
to 1 Hour 12 Minutes
Makes 6 appetizer servings

Sausage Crescents

⅓ cup onion, chopped
½ lb. bulk pork sausage
1 tablespoon catsup
½ teaspoon Italian
   seasoning
¼ teaspoon garlic powder
1 teaspoon lemon juice
1 (8 oz.) pkg. refrigerated
   crescent rolls
1 egg, beaten

In 1-quart casserole, combine onion and sausage. Microwave at HIGH (10) 4 to 5 minutes until sausage is browned; stir after 2 minutes to crumble sausage. Drain. Stir in catsup, Italian seasoning, garlic powder and lemon juice. Set aside to cool. Place metal accessory rack on turntable. Preheat oven to 375°F. Cut pastry into 4 rectangles. Divide sausage mixture into fourths. Spread sausage mixture down center of dough. Brush long edges of pastry with beaten egg and fold over to seal, enclosing sausage completely. Brush dough with beaten egg. Cut each length into 1-inch pieces. Arrange on greased 12-inch pizza pan. Convection Bake 10 to 13 minutes.

Total Convection Cooking Time 10 to 13 Minutes
Makes 24 appetizers

Spread sausage mixture down the center of dough.

Artichoke Dip

1 (14-oz.) can artichoke
   hearts, drained and
   finely chopped
1 cup mayonnaise
1 cup grated Parmesan
   cheese
¼ teaspoon garlic salt
Paprika

In 8-inch square glass baking dish, combine artichokes, mayonnaise, Parmesan cheese and garlic salt. Sprinkle with paprika. Microwave at HIGH (10) 3 to 5 minutes until heated through; stir after 2 minutes.

TO COOK BY CONVECTION: Place metal accessory rack on turntable. Preheat oven to 350°F. Convection Bake 15 to 20 minutes until heated through and top is light brown.

Total Microwave Cooking Time 3 to 5 Minutes
Total Convection Cooking Time 15 to 20 Minutes
Makes 2 cups

Cut each roll into 1-inch slices and place on pizza pan.

Tiny Chicken Turnovers

½ (8 oz.) pkg. cream cheese,
   softened
½ cup butter, softened
1 cup all-purpose flour
1 cup cooked chicken,
   finely chopped
1 tablespoon onion, finely
   chopped
1 tablespoon sweet red
   pepper, finely chopped
2 tablespoons mayonnaise
1 teaspoon Dijon mustard
¼ teaspoon salt
⅛ teaspoon white pepper
1 egg, beaten

Beat cream cheese and butter together until light and fluffy. Blend in flour to make a soft dough. Turn out onto floured surface and knead lightly 10 to 12 strokes. Wrap in plastic wrap and refrigerate until firm enough to handle.

Combine chicken, onion, red pepper, mayonnaise, mustard, salt and pepper; blend thoroughly. Set aside.

Roll out dough on well-floured surface to ⅟₁₆-inch thickness. Cut into 3-inch rounds. Place one heaping teaspoon filling on each pastry round. Brush edges of pastry with egg. Fold pastry rounds in half over filling. Seal edges together with a fork. Brush tops with remaining egg. Place metal accessory rack on turntable. Preheat oven to 400°F. Convection Bake 18 to 23 minutes until golden.

Total Convection Cooking Time 18 to 23 Minutes
Makes 20 appetizers

Appetizers & Beverages

Hot Cheese Dip

¼ cup onion, finely
    chopped
1 tablespoon butter
1 teaspoon cornstarch
¼ teaspoon pepper
½ cup whipping cream
2 teaspoons Worcestershire
    sauce
1 teaspoon soy sauce
2 cups American cheese,
    shredded
1 (3 oz.) pkg. cream cheese,
    softened
2 teaspoons parsley,
    snipped
Assorted chips or vegetable
    dippers

In 1½-quart casserole, combine onion and butter. Microwave at HIGH (10) 2 to 3 minutes until onion is tender. Blend in cornstarch, pepper, cream, Worcestershire sauce and soy sauce. Microwave at HIGH (10) 1 to 2 minutes until slightly thickened and bubbly, stirring every minute. Add cheese, cream cheese and parsley. Microwave at HIGH (10) 3 to 5 minutes until cheese is melted and mixture is heated through, stirring every minute.

Beer Cheese Dip: Prepare Hot Cheese Dip as above, substituting ¾ cup beer for cream.

Chili con Queso Dip: Prepare Hot Cheese Dip as above, substituting 1 cup shredded Monterey Jack cheese for American cheese. Add 4 oz. can mild chopped green chili peppers and ⅛ teaspoon hot sauce. Before serving, stir in 1 medium tomato, peeled, seeded and finely chopped.

Total Microwave Cooking Time 6 to 10 Minutes
Makes 8 servings

Brie In Pastry

Wrap dough over cheese to completely enclose. Moisten edges with water to seal.

1 sheet (half of a 17¼ oz.
    pkg.) puff pastry, thawed
    and unfolded
1 (14 to 18 oz.) round of
    Brie cheese
1 egg, beaten

Roll pastry to form a 12-inch square. Cut a 1-inch strip from each side of square. Roll 3 of the strips to 18-inch length and braid or twist to make 1 strip; set aside.

Place Brie, top down, in center of dough. Wrap dough over cheese, enclosing completely. Moisten edges of dough with water; seal well. Place sealed-side down on pizza pan. Moisten bottom edge of dough and gently press braid around side; press ends together to seal. Use remaining strip of dough to make decorative cutouts for top. Brush dough lightly with egg.

Place metal accessory rack on turntable. Preheat oven to 400°F. Convection Bake 18 to 23 minutes until pastry is puffed and lightly browned. Let stand 30 minutes before serving.

Total Convection Cooking Time 18 to 23 Minutes
Makes 1 round

Gently press braid around side and press ends to seal.

Sugar Glazed Walnuts

½ cup butter, melted
1 cup brown sugar, packed
1 teaspoon cinnamon
1 lb. walnut halves
    (about 4 cups)

In 1½-quart casserole, combine butter, brown sugar and cinnamon. Microwave at HIGH (10) 2 to 3 minutes; stir after 1 minute. Add nuts; mix to coat. Microwave at HIGH (10) 3 to 5 minutes. Spread on wax paper and cool slightly. Refrigerate in airtight container.

Total Microwave Cooking Time 5 to 8 Minutes
Makes 1 pound

Hot Chocolate

⅔ cup sugar
½ cup water
4 (1 oz.) squares
    unsweetened chocolate,
    cut up
5 cups milk

In 2-quart casserole, combine sugar, water and chocolate. Microwave at HIGH (10) 1 to 2 minutes until chocolate is melted; stir after 45 seconds with a wire whisk. Blend in milk. Microwave at HIGH (10) 6 to 9 minutes until hot, stirring every 3 minutes.

Peppermint Hot Chocolate: Prepare Hot Chocolate as above; stir in 1 or 2 drops Peppermint Schnapps after melting the chocolate.

S'more Hot Chocolate: Prepare Hot Chocolate as above; stir in ⅛ cup marshmallow creme after melting the chocolate.

Irish Hot Chocolate: Prepare Hot Chocolate as above; stir in ⅛ cup Irish Creme Liqueur after melting the chocolate.

Total Microwave Cooking Time 7 to 11 Minutes
Makes 4 (6 oz.) servings

Vary the flavor of Hot Chocolate by adding marshmallow creme or a flavored liqueur.

Zippy Tomato Cocktail

1 (12 oz.) can vegetable
    juice cocktail
½ cup beef broth
1 tablespoon lemon juice
1 teaspoon Worcestershire
    sauce
¼ teaspoon prepared
    horseradish
2 drops hot sauce

In 4-cup glass measure, combine vegetable juice cocktail, beef broth, lemon juice, Worcestershire sauce, horseradish and hot sauce. Microwave at HIGH (10) 7 to 9 minutes until hot; stir after 4 minutes.

Total Microwave Cooking Time 7 to 9 Minutes
Makes 2 (8 oz.) servings

Irish Coffee

2 to 3 cups strong coffee
4 teaspoons sugar
6 oz. Irish whiskey
Sweetened whipped cream

Pour ½ to ¾ cup coffee in each of 4 (10 to 12 oz.) cups. Microwave at HIGH (10) 3 to 4 minutes. For each drink, stir in 1 teaspoon sugar and 1½ ounces Irish whiskey; top with whipped cream.

Total Microwave Cooking Time 3 to 4 Minutes
Makes 4 servings

Hot Buttered Rum

4 cups apple juice
4 cinnamon sticks
4 tablespoons brown sugar,
    packed
4 oz. rum
4 teaspoons butter
Dash nutmeg

In each of 4 (10 to 12 oz.) mugs, combine 1 cup apple juice, 1 cinnamon stick and 1 tablespoon sugar. Microwave at HIGH (10) 3 to 4 minutes. For each drink stir in 1 oz. rum; top with 1 teaspoon butter and dash nutmeg.

Total Microwave Cooking Time 3 to 4 Minutes
Makes 4 servings

Soups & Stews

Minestrone Soup

1½ lbs. lean stew beef, cut
    into ½-inch cubes
5 cups hot water
1 medium onion, chopped
1 clove garlic, minced
1 teaspoon basil
¼ teaspoon pepper
1 (14½ oz.) can tomatoes
2 bay leaves
2 cups pasta, one-inch in
    length, uncooked
1½ cups small zucchini,
    sliced ¼-inch thick
1 cup cabbage, finely
    shredded
1 (10 oz.) pkg. frozen green
    beans, thawed
½ cup celery, chopped
2 tablespoons fresh parsley,
    snipped
½ teaspoon salt
1 (9 oz.) pkg. frozen baby
    carrots
1 (16 oz.) can navy beans

In 3-quart casserole, place beef, water, onion, garlic, basil, pepper, tomatoes and bay leaves. Cover. Microwave at HIGH (10) 20 to 25 minutes until meat is tender. Add pasta, zucchini, cabbage, green beans, celery, parsley and salt. Cover. Microwave at HIGH (10) 14 to 17 minutes until vegetables and pasta are tender. Add baby carrots and navy beans. Cover. Microwave at HIGH (10) 10 to 12 minutes; stir after 5 minutes. Discard bay leaves. Cover and let stand 5 minutes before serving.

Total Microwave Cooking Time 44 to 54 Minutes
Makes 8 to 10 servings

Cheese Soup with Broccoli, Cauliflower and Sausage

2 tablespoons butter
½ lb. smoked beef sausage
    or kielbasa, cubed
1 medium onion, chopped
½ teaspoon caraway seed
Dash pepper
1 bay leaf
2 (14½ oz.) cans chicken
    broth
3 medium potatoes, peeled
    and sliced
1½ cups broccoli flowerets
1½ cups cauliflower
    flowerets
¼ cup milk
1½ cups sharp Cheddar
    cheese, shredded

In 2-quart casserole, place butter, sausage, onion, caraway seed, pepper and bay leaf. Microwave at HIGH (10) 4 to 6 minutes until sausage begins to brown and onion is tender, stirring every 2 minutes. Add chicken broth, potatoes, broccoli and cauliflower. Microwave at MEDIUM HIGH (7) 28 to 32 minutes until vegetables are tender, stirring every 7 minutes. Stir in milk and Microwave at HIGH (10) 4 to 6 minutes until heated through. Discard bay leaf. Add cheese and stir until completely melted. Serve immediately.

Total Microwave Cooking Time 36 to 44 Minutes
Makes 2 to 4 servings

Soups & Stews

▲ *Beef Stew*

Beef Stew

1 small onion, sliced
1 clove garlic, minced
2 cups water
1 (1¾ oz.) pkg. dry onion-
  mushroom soup mix
1 teaspoon thyme
½ teaspoon salt
½ teaspoon pepper
2 lbs. boneless beef chuck,
  cut into ½-inch cubes
2 cups potatoes, peeled and
  cubed
½ (16 oz.) pkg. baby carrots
3 tablespoons cornstarch
¼ cup water
½ (16 oz.) pkg. frozen cut
  green beans

In 3-quart casserole, place onion, garlic, 2 cups water, onion soup mix, thyme, salt and pepper. Add meat; stir to coat. Cover. Microwave at MEDIUM HIGH (7) 35 minutes; stir after 15 minutes. Add potatoes and carrots. Cover. Microwave at MEDIUM HIGH (7) 30 minutes until meat and vegetables are tender, stirring after 15 minutes.

In 2-cup measure, combine cornstarch with ¼ cup water, stirring to blend well. Add cornstarch mixture and green beans to stew; stir until blended. Cover. Microwave at HIGH (10) 7 to 10 minutes until thickened; stir after 3 minutes.

Total Microwave Cooking Time 1 hour 12 Minutes
to 1 hour 15 Minutes
Makes 6 to 8 servings

Cheddar Broccoli Soup

2 lbs. broccoli, chopped
2 tablespoons butter
½ cup onion, chopped
¼ cup green pepper,
    chopped
2 tablespoons fresh parsley,
    chopped
1 bay leaf
1 teaspoon thyme
¼ teaspoon salt
6 black peppercorns
⅛ teaspoon nutmeg
2 (14½ oz.) cans chicken
    broth
¼ cup all-purpose flour
3 egg yolks, beaten
1 cup milk
1 cup sharp Cheddar
    cheese, shredded

In 3-quart casserole, combine broccoli, butter, onion, green pepper, parsley, bay leaf, thyme, salt, peppercorns and nutmeg. Cover. Microwave at HIGH (10) 8 to 10 minutes until broccoli is tender; stir after 4 minutes. Discard bay leaf. Spoon mixture into blender. Add 1 can chicken broth. Blend for 1 minute on low speed.

Blend flour and remaining broth in 3-quart casserole. Stir well with a wire whisk. Add broccoli mixture; stir to blend. Microwave at HIGH (10) 10 to 12 minutes; stir after 5 minutes.

In 1-quart casserole, blend eggs and milk. Gradually add egg mixture to soup, stirring constantly. Add cheese. Microwave at HIGH (10) 4 minutes until cheese is completely melted, stirring after 2 minutes.

Total Microwave Cooking Time 22 to 26 Minutes
Makes 4 to 6 servings

Combine cooked vegetables and seasonings in a blender.

Burgundy Beef Stew

4 slices bacon, diced
1 large onion, chopped
2 medium carrots, sliced
    ¼-inch thick
3 cloves garlic, finely
    chopped
1½ cups Burgundy wine
¼ cup brandy
1½ teaspoons thyme
1 teaspoon oregano
1 teaspoon salt
½ teaspoon pepper
3 lbs. boneless beef chuck,
    cut into 1-inch cubes
1 (8 oz.) pkg. frozen small
    whole onions
½ lb. fresh mushrooms,
    quartered
¼ cup water
¼ cup all-purpose flour
Cooked noodles
    (optional)

In 3-quart casserole, place bacon, onion, carrots and garlic. Cover. Microwave at HIGH (10) 5 to 7 minutes until bacon is cooked and vegetables are tender; stir after 3 minutes. Drain. Blend in wine, brandy, thyme, oregano, salt and pepper. Add meat and stir to coat. Microwave at MEDIUM (5) 29 to 31 minutes. Add onions and mushrooms. Microwave at MEDIUM (5) 15 to 20 minutes until meat and vegetables are tender, stirring every 5 minutes.

In 1-cup measure blend water and flour to make a smooth paste. Stir into stew. Cover. Microwave at HIGH (10) 5 to 7 minutes; stir after 3 minutes. Serve over noodles, if desired.

Total Microwave Cooking Time 54 to 65 Minutes
Makes 8 to 10 servings

Soups & Stews

Cheesy Vegetable Soup

1 cup water
1 large potato, shredded
1 small onion, finely
    chopped
3 small carrots, grated
1 stalk celery, finely
    chopped
1 cup chicken broth
½ cup half & half
1½ cups sharp Cheddar
    cheese, shredded
Dash salt
Dash white pepper

In 2-quart casserole, combine water, potato, onion, carrots and celery. Cover. Microwave at HIGH (10) 10 to 12 minutes until potatoes are tender; stir after 5 minutes. Blend in chicken broth and half & half. Cover. Microwave at MEDIUM HIGH (7) 6 to 8 minutes until heated through. Add cheese, salt and pepper; stir until cheese is completely melted.

Total Microwave Cooking Time 16 to 20 Minutes
Makes 4 servings

Creamy Mushroom Soup

Coarsely chop stems and add to broth for flavor.

2 lbs. fresh mushrooms
2 (14½ oz.) cans chicken
    broth
1 (1¾ oz.) pkg. dry onion
    soup mix
3 tablespoons butter, sliced
3 tablespoons all-purpose
    flour
1 cup half & half
3 egg yolks
¼ cup sherry
Dash hot sauce
Dash pepper

Thinly slice mushroom caps and set aside. Coarsely chop stems and place in 4-cup glass measure. Add 1 can of chicken broth. Microwave at HIGH (10) 8 minutes until broth is brown. Strain broth into 3-quart casserole; discard mushroom pieces. Add soup mix, remaining chicken broth, mushroom caps and butter. Microwave at HIGH (10) 15 to 18 minutes, uncovered; stir after 7 minutes. In 4-cup glass measure, combine flour, half & half and egg yolks; stir until smooth. Gradually add cream mixture, sherry, hot sauce and pepper to hot soup, stirring constantly with a wire whisk. Microwave at HIGH (10) 7 to 10 minutes until slightly thickened, stirring every 4 minutes.

Total Microwave Cooking Time 30 to 36 Minutes
Makes 6 to 8 servings

Chicken Noodle Soup

Strain broth and discard mushroom pieces before adding the soup mix.

2 lbs. chicken pieces
4 celery stalks, cut up
2 bay leaves
2 teaspoons peppercorns
1 teaspoon salt
1 onion, sliced
6 cups hot water
3 carrots, shredded
1 to 1½ cups egg noodles,
    uncooked

In 3-quart casserole, combine chicken, celery, bay leaves, peppercorns, salt, onion and water. Cover. Microwave at HIGH (10) 10 minutes. Stir. Continue to Microwave at MEDIUM (5) 35 to 37 minutes until chicken is tender. Remove chicken from broth; set aside to cool. Add carrots and noodles to broth. Remove chicken from bone, coarsely chop and add to broth. Cover. Microwave at MEDIUM HIGH (7) 7 to 8 minutes until noodles and carrots are tender. Discard bay leaves.

Total Microwave Cooking Time 52 to 55 Minutes
Makes 8 servings

Chili

1 lb. ground chuck
1 medium onion, chopped
½ cup green pepper, chopped
1 (14½ oz.) can whole tomatoes, chopped
1 (15½ oz.) can kidney beans
1 (6 oz.) can tomato paste
½ cup water
2 teaspoons chili powder
1 teaspoon garlic salt
1 teaspoon oregano
½ teaspoon cumin
½ teaspoon cayenne pepper

In 2-quart casserole, combine ground chuck, onion and green pepper. Cover. Microwave at HIGH (10) 4 to 6 minutes until meat is browned, stirring every 2 minutes. Drain. Add tomatoes, kidney beans, tomato paste, water, chili powder, garlic salt, oregano, cumin and cayenne pepper; stir to blend. Cover. Microwave at MEDIUM HIGH (7) 20 to 25 minutes, stirring every 7 minutes. Let stand, covered, 5 minutes before serving.

Total Microwave Cooking Time 24 to 31 Minutes
Makes 4 to 6 servings

French Onion Soup

¼ cup butter
4 medium onions, thinly sliced
3 cloves garlic, minced
2 (10½ oz.) cans beef broth
½ cup water
2 tablespoons dry sherry
½ teaspoon salt
⅛ teaspoon fresh ground pepper
4 to 5 slices French bread
1 to 1½ cups Swiss cheese, shredded

In 3-quart casserole, place butter, onions and garlic. Microwave at HIGH (10) 5 to 8 minutes until onions are tender. Add beef broth, water, sherry, salt and pepper; stir to blend. Microwave at HIGH (10) 10 to 12 minutes.

Top individual servings with one slice of French bread; sprinkle with cheese. Microwave at HIGH (10) 30 to 45 seconds until cheese is completely melted.

Total Microwave Cooking Time 15½ to 20¾ Minutes
Makes 4 to 5 servings

Add cheese for topping and microwave.

Clam Chowder

2 tablespoons onion, finely chopped
1 tablespoon vegetable oil
1 small potato, peeled and cubed
½ cup water
½ teaspoon seasoned salt
Dash pepper
1 tablespoon all-purpose flour
1 cup milk, divided
1 (6½ oz.) can minced clams, undrained
1 tablespoon butter

In 2-quart casserole, combine onion and oil. Microwave at HIGH (10) 2 to 3 minutes until onion is tender. Add potatoes, water, seasoned salt and pepper. Cover. Microwave at HIGH (10) 5 to 6 minutes until potatoes are tender; stir after 2 minutes. Add flour to ¼ cup milk; stir well to blend. Add flour mixture, remaining milk, clams and butter to potatoes and onions. Microwave at HIGH (10) 6 to 8 minutes, stirring every 2 minutes.

Total Microwave Cooking Time 13 to 17 Minutes
Makes 3 servings

Meats

Flank Steak Florentine

1½ to 1¾ lb. beef flank
    steak
½ cup fresh mushrooms,
    chopped
1 medium onion, chopped
1 small carrot, finely
    chopped
1 clove garlic, minced
3 tablespoons butter
1 (10 oz.) pkg. frozen
    chopped spinach,
    thawed and well drained
2 teaspoons instant beef
    bouillon granules
¼ cup hot water
1 (10¾ oz.) can cream of
    chicken soup
2 tablespoons capers,
    drained
2 tablespoons dry vermouth
    (optional)
½ teaspoon curry powder
¼ teaspoon coriander
¼ teaspoon white pepper

Pound flank steak with a meat mallet to ⅛-inch thickness; score with a sharp knife. In 1½-quart casserole, combine mushrooms, onion, carrot, garlic, butter and spinach. Cover. Microwave at HIGH (10) 4 to 6 minutes. Spread spinach mixture over steak. Starting at long side, roll steak in jelly roll fashion. Tie with string or secure with toothpicks.

Place steak, seam side up, in 2-quart oblong glass baking dish. In 4-cup glass measure, dissolve bouillon granules in hot water. Add soup, capers, vermouth, curry powder, coriander and pepper. Pour over steak; cover. Place metal accessory rack on turntable. Preheat oven to 325°F. Cook on Combination 60 to 70 minutes until tender; turn meat over after 40 minutes.

TO COOK BY MICROWAVE: Cover with vented plastic wrap. Microwave at HIGH (10) 10 minutes. Microwave at LOW (3) 40 to 45 minutes; turn steak over after 20 minutes. Let stand, covered, 10 minutes.

> Total Combination Cooking Time 60 to 70 Minutes
> Total Microwave Cooking Time 54 to 61 Minutes
> Makes 4 servings

Barbecued Beef Brisket

1 cup catsup
2 tablespoons
    Worcestershire sauce
1 tablespoon Dijon mustard
1 tablespoon red wine
    vinegar
1 tablespoon brown sugar
½ teaspoon salt
¼ teaspoon garlic salt
¼ teaspoon celery salt
⅛ teaspoon cayenne pepper
1 (3 to 4 lb.) beef brisket

In small bowl, combine catsup, Worcestershire sauce, mustard, vinegar, sugar, salt, garlic salt, celery salt and cayenne pepper. Pierce brisket in several places on both sides with a fork. Place in 2-quart oblong glass baking dish. Pour half of sauce over brisket; cover loosely with plastic wrap.

Microwave at HIGH (10) 15 minutes. Microwave at MEDIUM (5) 40 minutes. Turn over and add remaining sauce. Cover. Microwave at MEDIUM (5) 45 to 50 minutes until tender. Let stand, covered, 10 minutes.

TO COOK BY COMBINATION: Place brisket in cooking bag following package directions. Add all of sauce. Place metal accessory rack on turntable. Preheat oven to 300°F. Cook on Combination 1¾ to 2¼ hours; carefully turn meat over after 1 hour.

> Total Microwave Cooking Time 1 Hour 40 Minutes
> to 1 Hour 50 Minutes
> Total Combination Cooking Time 1¾ to 2¼ Hours
> Makes 6 to 8 servings

▲ *Beef Rib Eye Roast with Mushroom Sauce*

Beef Rib Eye Roast with Mushroom Sauce

1 cup water
¼ cup bourbon
1 tablespoon lemon juice
1 tablespoon steak sauce
½ teaspoon garlic salt
½ teaspoon lemon pepper
   seasoning
¼ teaspoon cayenne pepper
1 (4 to 5 lb.) beef rib eye
   roast
½ lb. sliced fresh
   mushrooms
½ cup water
2 teaspoons instant beef
   bouillon granules
2 teaspoons browning sauce
2 tablespoons cornstarch
¼ cup water

In 4-cup glass measure, combine 1 cup water, bourbon, lemon juice, steak sauce, garlic salt, lemon pepper and cayenne pepper. Pierce roast with a fork in several places. Place meat in 2-quart oblong glass baking dish. Pour marinade over roast and cover. Marinate in refrigerator 8 hours, turning occasionally. Drain and reserve ½ cup marinade.

Place metal accessory rack on turntable. Place roast on trivet in 2-quart oblong glass baking dish. Preheat oven to 300°F. Cook on Combination to desired doneness according to directions in chart, page 137.

Mushroom Sauce: In 1½-quart casserole, combine reserved marinade, mushrooms, ½ cup water, bouillon granules and browning sauce. Microwave at HIGH (10) 2 to 3 minutes. Combine cornstarch and ¼ cup water; stir into mushroom mixture. Microwave at HIGH (10) 2 to 3 minutes until thickened, stirring every minute.

Makes 10 to 12 servings

Cheese-Stuffed Meat Loaf

1½ cups soft bread crumbs
1 egg, slightly beaten
½ teaspoon seasoned salt
¼ teaspoon pepper
¼ cup milk
¾ cup onion, finely
    chopped, divided
1½ lbs. ground round
2 tablespoons green
    pepper, minced
2 tablespoons celery,
    minced
1 (2 oz.) jar sliced
    pimento, well drained
1 teaspoon lemon juice
1 egg, slightly beaten
1 cup Cheddar cheese,
    finely shredded
½ cup soft bread crumbs

In large mixing bowl, combine 1½ cups bread crumbs, 1 egg, seasoned salt, pepper, milk, ½ cup onion and ground round.

In 1½-quart casserole, combine ¼ cup onion, green pepper, celery, pimento and lemon juice. Microwave at HIGH (10) 2 to 3 minutes until crisp-tender. Add egg; blend well. Stir in cheese and ½ cup bread crumbs.

On strip of wax paper, shape meat mixture into a 14x7-inch rectangle. Spread cheese mixture over meat to within 1 inch of edges. Lifting wax paper for support, roll meat mixture from short side in jelly roll fashion. Place seam-side down in 9x5-inch glass loaf dish. Cover with vented plastic wrap. Microwave at MEDIUM HIGH (7) 23 to 26 minutes. Add topping (see below) and Microwave, uncovered, at MEDIUM HIGH (7) 3 to 4 minutes. Let stand 5 minutes.

Spicy Tomato Topping: In small bowl, combine ½ cup catsup, 3 tablespoons brown sugar, ½ teaspoon dry mustard and ¼ teaspoon allspice.

TO COOK BY COMBINATION: Place metal accessory rack on turntable. Do not cover meat loaf. Preheat oven to 325°F. Cook on Combination 35 to 40 minutes. Add topping and continue cooking 5 minutes.

Total Microwave Cooking Time 26 to 30 Minutes
Total Combination Cooking Time 40 to 45 Minutes
Makes 6 servings

Spread cheese mixture over meat within one-inch from sides.

Carefully roll up meat mixture from the short side.

Marinated Pot Roast

1 (2½ to 3 lb.) boneless
    chuck roast
1 cup zesty Italian salad
    dressing
1 teaspoon pepper
½ teaspoon salt
¼ teaspoon garlic powder
Water
½ (8 oz.) pkg. fresh
    baby-cut carrots
1 cup sliced fresh
    mushrooms

Pierce roast on both sides with a fork. Place in zip-top plastic bag. Combine salad dressing, pepper, salt and garlic powder; pour over roast. Seal bag and refrigerate 6 to 8 hours, or overnight, turning occasionally.

Drain meat, reserving ⅛ cup marinade; add enough water to reserved marinade to make 1 cup. Place meat and marinade mixture in 2-quart oblong glass baking dish; cover. Microwave at HIGH (10) 10 minutes. Microwave at LOW (3) 60 minutes; turn roast over after 25 minutes. Add carrots and mushrooms. Cover and Microwave at MEDIUM (5) 12 to 15 minutes until vegetables are tender.

Total Microwave Cooking Time 1 Hour 22 Minutes
to 1 Hour 25 Minutes
Makes 6 servings

Pierce roast with a fork to allow seasonings to penetrate before marinating.

Meats

Scandinavian Meatballs

For evenly shaped meatballs, use an ice cream scoop to divide meat mixture.

1 lb. ground chuck
½ lb. ground veal
½ lb. ground pork
2 cups soft bread crumbs
½ cup milk
1 egg
1 (1¾ oz.) pkg. dry onion soup mix
½ teaspoon pepper
¼ teaspoon nutmeg
1 teaspoon instant beef bouillon granules
1 cup hot water
3 tablespoons all-purpose flour
1 cup half & half

Mix together ground meats, bread crumbs, milk, egg, onion soup mix, pepper and nutmeg. Shape into 24 meatballs. Place meatballs in 2-quart oblong glass baking dish. Cover with wax paper. Microwave at HIGH (10) 14 to 17 minutes, rearranging meatballs after 8 minutes. Remove meatballs to warm platter. Reserve ¼ cup drippings and return to dish.

Dissolve bouillon granules in hot water. Add flour to reserved drippings; stir until smooth. Gradually stir in bouillon and half & half. Microwave at HIGH (10) 4 to 5 minutes until thickened, stirring every 2 minutes. Return meatballs to dish; turn over to coat evenly. Microwave at HIGH (10) 2 to 3 minutes until hot. Serve over noodles.

Total Microwave Cooking Time 20 to 25 Minutes
Makes 8 servings

Savory Swiss Steak

1½ lbs. boneless round steak, pounded ¼-inch thick
1 (14½ oz.) can stewed tomatoes
1 (8 oz.) can tomato sauce
1 (1¾ oz.) pkg. dry onion-mushroom soup mix
2 tablespoons fresh parsley, snipped
1 tablespoon Worcestershire sauce
1 teaspoon basil

Cut steak into serving size portions. In 3-quart casserole, combine tomatoes, tomato sauce, soup mix, parsley, Worcestershire sauce and basil. Add steak, submerging in tomato mixture. Cover. Microwave at HIGH (10) 5 minutes and at MEDIUM (5) 35 to 40 minutes. Let stand, covered, 5 minutes before serving.

TO COOK BY COMBINATION: Place metal accessory rack on turntable. Preheat oven to 300°F. Cook on Combination 55 to 60 minutes until tender. Let stand, covered, 5 minutes before serving.

Total Microwave Cooking Time 38 to 43 Minutes
Total Combination Cooking Time 55 to 60 Minutes
Makes 4 to 6 servings

Taco Salad

1½ lbs. ground chuck
½ cup onion, chopped
1 cup green pepper, chopped
1 (16 oz.) can hot chili beans in chili gravy
1 (10 oz.) can mild enchilada sauce
1 (15 oz.) can tomato sauce
1 (10 oz.) pkg. corn chips
1 cup Cheddar cheese, shredded, divided
4 cups lettuce, shredded
2 cups tomatoes, chopped

In 1½-quart casserole, crumble beef. Add onion and green pepper; cover. Microwave at HIGH (10) 6 to 8 minutes; stir after 3 minutes. Drain well. Add chili beans. Cover. Microwave at HIGH (10) 4 to 6 minutes until hot. Set aside and keep warm.

In 2-quart casserole, combine enchilada sauce and tomato sauce. Microwave at HIGH (10) 5 to 6 minutes; stir after 3 minutes.

In large salad bowl, layer corn chips, meat mixture, half of cheese, lettuce and tomatoes. Top with sauce and sprinkle with remaining cheese. Serve immediately.

Total Microwave Cooking Time 15 to 20 Minutes
Makes 6 to 8 servings

Stuffed Peppers

▲ Stuffed Peppers

4 medium yellow, green or
  red peppers
1 lb. ground chuck
½ cup onion, chopped
⅓ cup celery, chopped
1 clove garlic, minced
1 (7½ oz.) can tomatoes
⅔ cup cooked rice
1 (2 oz.) jar sliced pimento,
  drained
¼ teaspoon pepper
1 (10¾ oz.) can tomato
  soup
½ teaspoon basil
¼ cup sharp Cheddar
  cheese, shredded

Cut off tops of peppers. Remove seeds and membrane;
set aside. In 1½-quart casserole, crumble beef. Add
onion, celery and garlic; cover. Microwave at HIGH
(10) 5 to 7 minutes; stir after 3 minutes. Drain well.
Combine meat mixture, tomatoes, rice, pimento and
pepper. Fill peppers with meat mixture. Place peppers
in a 2-quart casserole. Combine soup and basil; pour
over peppers. Cover. Microwave at HIGH (10) 15 to 18
minutes. Sprinkle cheese over peppers. Let stand,
covered, 5 minutes.

TO COOK BY COMBINATION: Place metal accessory
rack on turntable. Preheat oven to 375°F. Cook on
Combination 27 to 30 minutes. Sprinkle with cheese
before serving.

Total Microwave Cooking Time 20 to 25 Minutes
Total Combination Cooking Time 27 to 30 Minutes
Makes 4 servings

Oriental Beef and Vegetables

1 lb. boneless top sirloin
  steak
1 clove garlic, minced
3 tablespoons soy sauce
3 tablespoons dry sherry
1 tablespoon cornstarch
1 teaspoon brown sugar
2 teaspoons sesame oil
1 (6 oz.) pkg. frozen pea
  pods, thawed
1 medium sweet red
  pepper, cut into strips
1 (8 oz.) can sliced water
  chestnuts, drained

Slice steak diagonally across grain into 2½ x ½-inch strips.
In medium bowl, combine garlic, soy sauce, sherry,
cornstarch and brown sugar. Add beef; mix well and
refrigerate 30 minutes. Drain, reserving marinade.

Place beef and oil in 2-quart oblong glass baking dish.
Cover with wax paper. Microwave at HIGH (10) 7 to 9
minutes until beef is no longer pink; stir after 5
minutes. Add reserved marinade, pea pods, red pepper
and water chestnuts. Cover. Microwave at HIGH (10)
7 to 9 minutes until sauce is thickened and vegetables
are crisp-tender; stir after 4 minutes.

Total Microwave Cooking Time 14 to 18 Minutes
Makes 4 to 6 servings

*Tuck wax paper under ends of dish
to hold securely in place.*

Meats

▲ *Glazed Pork Roast*
with Pineapple Salsa

Glazed Pork Roast with Pineapple Salsa

2 cups fresh pineapple,
finely chopped
1 small sweet red pepper,
finely chopped
1 small green pepper,
finely chopped
1 small red onion,
finely chopped
3 tablespoons fresh
parsley, snipped
2 tablespoons fresh chives,
snipped
2 tablespoons lemon juice
1 teaspoon vegetable oil
¼ teaspoon cayenne pepper
1 (4 to 5 lb.) pork loin roast

Combine pineapple, green and red pepper, onion, parsley, chives, lemon juice, oil and cayenne pepper. Cover and refrigerate 2 hours.

Place metal accessory rack on turntable. Preheat oven to 300°F. Place roast on trivet in 2-quart oblong glass baking dish. Cook pork roast according to directions in chart, page 137. During last 5 minutes of cooking time, baste roast occasionally with Pineapple Glaze. Serve with salsa.

Pineapple Glaze: Combine ½ cup pineapple preserves, 1 tablespoon orange juice, ¼ teaspoon cinnamon and ⅛ teaspoon ginger.

Makes 6 to 8 servings

Classic Ham Loaf

1 lb. ground cooked ham
½ lb. ground fresh pork
½ cup soft bread crumbs
½ cup water
1 egg
½ cup onion,
finely chopped
¼ teaspoon pepper
¼ teaspoon marjoram

Combine all ingredients. Place in 9x5-inch glass loaf dish. Cover with vented plastic wrap. Microwave at MEDIUM HIGH (7) 23 to 27 minutes. Let stand 5 minutes before serving.

TO COOK BY COMBINATION: Place metal accessory rack on turntable. Preheat oven to 350°F. Do not cover dish. Cook on Combination 30 to 37 minutes. Let stand 5 minutes.

Total Microwave Cooking Time 23 to 27 Minutes
Total Combination Cooking Time 30 to 37 Minutes
Makes 6 servings

Italian Sloppy Joes

1½ lbs. mild bulk Italian
    sausage
½ cup onion, chopped
½ cup green pepper,
    chopped
1 (2¼ oz.) can sliced ripe
    olives, drained
1 (28 oz.) can whole
    tomatoes, drained and
    chopped
½ teaspoon oregano
¼ teaspoon salt
¼ teaspoon pepper
3 hamburger buns, split and
    toasted
½ cup mozzarella cheese,
    shredded

In 2-quart casserole, crumble sausage. Add onion and green pepper; cover. Microwave at HIGH (10) 8 to 10 minutes; stir after 4 minutes. Drain well. Add olives, tomatoes, oregano, salt and pepper. Microwave at HIGH (10) 4 to 6 minutes until hot.

Serve over hamburger buns. Sprinkle with mozzarella cheese.

Total Microwave Cooking Time 12 to 16 Minutes
Makes 6 servings

When microwaving sausage, use a microwave-safe colander inside the casserole dish to eliminate draining.

Sweet and Sour Ham

1 (20 oz.) can pineapple
    chunks
1 (10½ oz.) can beef broth
3 tablespoons cornstarch
2 cups cooked ham, cut into
    1-inch cubes
1 small green pepper,
    cut into strips
1 small sweet red pepper,
    cut into strips
1 small onion,
    thinly sliced
¾ teaspoon dry mustard
2 tablespoons brown sugar
3 tablespoons vinegar
Chinese noodles or rice

Drain pineapple, reserving ⅓ cup juice. In 3-quart casserole, combine reserved juice, beef broth and cornstarch; stir until smooth. Microwave at HIGH (10) 3 to 5 minutes until thickened; stir after 2 minutes.

Add pineapple chunks, ham, peppers, onion, dry mustard, brown sugar and vinegar. Micro-wave at HIGH (10) 5 to 6 minutes until vegetables are crisp-tender. Serve over Chinese noodles or rice.

Total Microwave Cooking Time 8 to 11 Minutes
Makes 4 servings

Lemon Pork Chops

4 rib pork chops,
    ¾-inch thick
½ teaspoon salt
¼ teaspoon pepper
¼ teaspoon thyme
½ cup chili sauce
1 tablespoon brown sugar
4 onion slices
4 lemon slices

Sprinkle chops with salt, pepper and thyme. Arrange chops in 2-quart casserole. Combine chili sauce and brown sugar; pour over chops. Place onion and lemon slice on each chop. Cover. Place metal accessory rack on turntable. Preheat oven to 350°F. Cook on Combination 32 to 37 minutes until tender.

TO COOK BY MICROWAVE: Microwave at MEDIUM HIGH (7) 18 to 23 minutes until tender.

Total Combination Cooking Time 32 to 37 Minutes
Total Microwave Cooking Time 18 to 23 Minutes
Makes 4 servings

Meats

Barbecued Spareribs

2½ to 3 lbs. spareribs,
  cut into 2-rib pieces
1 medium onion, chopped
1 medium sweet red
  pepper, chopped
2 cloves garlic, minced
½ cup catsup
½ cup brown sugar, packed
¼ cup molasses
2 tablespoons lemon juice
1 teaspoon Dijon mustard
Dash hot sauce

Place ribs in 3-quart casserole; cover. Microwave at MEDIUM (5) 30 minutes. In small mixing bowl, combine onion, red pepper, garlic, catsup, sugar, molasses, lemon juice, mustard and hot sauce. Turn ribs over and add sauce. Cover and Microwave at MEDIUM (5) 40 to 45 minutes. Let stand 5 minutes.

TO COOK BY COMBINATION: Place metal accessory rack on turntable. Preheat oven to 350°F. Cook on Combination 1 to 1¼ hours; baste with sauce during last 30 minutes.

Total Microwave Cooking Time 1 Hour 10 Minutes
to 1 Hour 15 Minutes
Total Combination Cooking Time 1 to 1¼ Hours
Makes 4 servings

Fruited Pork Tenderloin

2 whole pork tenderloins
  (about 2 lbs. total)
¼ cup butter, melted
1 cup Madeira wine
1 tablespoon molasses
1 teaspoon thyme
¼ teaspoon garlic powder
½ cup pitted prunes
½ cup dried apricots

Place tenderloins in 2-quart oblong glass baking dish. In small bowl, combine butter, wine, molasses, thyme and garlic powder. Pour over tenderloins. Cover and marinate in refrigerator 6 to 8 hours or overnight.

Place metal accessory rack on turntable. Preheat oven to 350°F. Cook on Combination 20 minutes. Turn tenderloins over and add prunes and apricots, making certain that fruit is submerged in liquid. Continue cooking on Combination 18 to 23 minutes until done. Let stand 5 minutes.

TO COOK BY CONVECTION: Place metal accessory rack on turntable. Preheat oven to 350°F. Convection Bake 50 to 55 minutes; add fruit during last 20 minutes of cooking time.

Total Combination Cooking Time 38 to 43 Minutes
Total Convection Cooking Time 50 to 55 Minutes
Makes 6 servings

Peachy Glazed Ham Slice

1 (8¾ oz.) can peach
  slices, drained
2 tablespoons honey
2 tablespoons lemon juice
¼ teaspoon allspice
1 teaspoon grated
  lemon rind
1 fully-cooked center ham
  slice, 1¼ inches thick

In container of electric blender, combine peach slices, honey, lemon juice and allspice. Cover and blend until smooth; stir in lemon rind.

Place ham in 1½-quart oblong glass baking dish. Cover with wax paper. Microwave at HIGH (10) 6 to 7 minutes. Uncover, brush with glaze. Microwave at HIGH (10) 2 to 3 minutes. Pour remaining glaze in 2-cup glass measure. Microwave at HIGH (10) 1 to 2 minutes until heated through. Spoon over ham.

Total Microwave Cooking Time 9 to 12 Minutes
Makes 6 to 8 servings

▲ *Apple-Stuffed Pork Chops*

Apple-Stuffed Pork Chops

¾ **cup herb-seasoned**
   stuffing mix
⅛ **cup apple, diced**
¼ **cup onion,**
   finely chopped
2 **tablespoons raisins,**
   coarsely chopped
¼ **cup orange juice**
1 **tablespoon butter, melted**
1 **tablespoon grated**
   orange rind
½ **teaspoon salt**
¼ **teaspoon cinnamon**
4 **center-cut pork chops,**
   1-inch thick
½ **cup apple jelly**
2 **tablespoons orange juice**

In mixing bowl, combine stuffing mix, apple, onion, raisins, ¼ cup orange juice, butter, orange rind, salt and cinnamon. Cut a pocket in each pork chop. Divide stuffing evenly among chops.

Arrange chops in 2-quart oblong glass baking dish with thickest meaty areas to outside edges. In 1-cup glass measure, combine jelly and 2 tablespoons orange juice. Microwave at HIGH (10) 1 to 2 minutes; stir well. Brush half of mixture over chops.

Place metal accessory rack on turntable. Preheat oven to 375°F. Cook on Combination 18 minutes. Turn chops over and brush with remaining sauce. Continue cooking 18 to 20 minutes until done.

TO COOK BY MICROWAVE: Cover with vented plastic wrap. Microwave at MEDIUM HIGH (7) 25 to 30 minutes, turning chops over after 15 minutes.

Total Combination Cooking Time 36 to 38 Minutes
Total Microwave Cooking Time 26 to 32 Minutes
Makes 4 servings

To form a pocket, use a sharp knife to cut pork chop through center.

Place the stuffing in pocket.

Meats

▲ *Veal Roll-Ups*

Tasty Veal Chops

6 veal loin chops,
   ¾-inch thick
¼ cup water
¼ cup dry sherry
2 tablespoons soy sauce
¼ teaspoon marjoram
¼ teaspoon pepper
½ cup water
2 tablespoons cornstarch
1 (4 oz.) can sliced
   mushrooms, drained
1 (8 oz.) can sliced water
   chestnuts, drained

Place chops in 3-quart casserole. Combine ¼ cup water, sherry, soy sauce, marjoram and pepper; pour over chops. Cover and let stand at room temperature 1 hour; turn once. Microwave, covered, at MEDIUM HIGH (7) 17 to 21 minutes until tender; turn over after 10 minutes. Remove chops to warm platter.

Combine ½ cup water and cornstarch; stir until smooth. Add to cooking liquid. Microwave at HIGH (10) 2 to 3 minutes until thickened, stirring every minute. Add mushrooms and water chestnuts. Microwave at HIGH (10) 2 to 3 minutes until hot. Spoon sauce over chops.

TO COOK BY COMBINATION: Place metal accessory rack on turntable. Preheat oven to 350°F. Cook on Combination 26 to 30 minutes. Microwave sauce as described above.

Total Microwave Cooking Time 21 to 27 Minutes
Total Combination Cooking Time 26 to 30 Minutes
Makes 6 servings

Veal Roll-Ups

6 boneless veal cutlets,
    ½-inch thick
6 thin slices Swiss cheese
6 thin slices boiled ham
2 eggs
¼ cup butter, melted
½ cup dry bread crumbs
¼ cup all-purpose flour
1 teaspoon salt
½ teaspoon paprika
¼ teaspoon onion powder
¼ teaspoon sage
¼ teaspoon pepper

Pound each cutlet with meat mallet to ¼-inch thickness. Place 1 slice cheese and 1 slice ham on each piece of veal. Roll up tightly and fasten with a toothpick.

In small bowl, beat together eggs and butter. In shallow dish, combine bread crumbs, flour, salt, paprika, onion powder, sage and pepper. Dip veal rolls in egg mixture, then roll in crumb mixture. Place rolls in 2-quart oblong glass baking dish. Place metal accessory rack on turntable. Preheat oven to 325°F. Cook on Combination 25 to 30 minutes.

Total Combination Cooking Time 25 to 30 Minutes
Makes 4 to 6 servings

Place cheese and ham on top of flattened veal cutlet.

Veal with Rosemary

1½ lbs. veal round steak,
    cut into strips
2 tablespoons butter
1 (4 oz.) jar sliced
    mushrooms
2 green onions, sliced
1 teaspoon rosemary,
    crushed
½ teaspoon salt
¼ teaspoon pepper
1 tablespoon cornstarch
¼ cup water
2 tomatoes, cut in wedges
2 tablespoons fresh
    parsley, snipped

Place veal, butter, mushrooms, onions, rosemary, salt and pepper in 2-quart casserole; cover. Microwave at MEDIUM HIGH (7) 20 minutes. Combine cornstarch and water; stir until smooth. Add to veal mixture. Microwave at HIGH (10) 2 to 3 minutes until thickened; stir after 1 minute. Add tomatoes and parsley. Microwave at HIGH (10) 2 minutes until hot. Serve over noodles or rice.

Total Microwave Cooking Time 24 to 25 Minutes
Makes 6 servings

Dip veal roll in egg mixture then roll in crumb mixture.

Leg of Lamb with Mustard Glaze

½ cup Dijon mustard
1 teaspoon basil
¼ teaspoon thyme
¼ teaspoon white pepper
2 tablespoons vegetable oil
2 tablespoons
    Worcestershire sauce
1 (4 to 5 lb.) leg of lamb

Combine mustard, basil, thyme, pepper, oil and Worcestershire sauce. Pierce lamb in several places with fork. Place fat side up on trivet in 2-quart oblong glass baking dish. Spread mustard mixture over lamb. Chill 2 hours.

TO COOK BY COMBINATION: Place metal accessory rack on turntable. Preheat oven to 300°F. Cook on Combination to desired doneness according to chart on page 137.

TO COOK BY CONVECTION: Place metal accessory rack on turntable. Preheat oven to 325°F. Convection Bake to desired doneness according to chart on page 136.

Makes 6 to 8 servings

Meats

▲ *Zesty Lamb Kabobs*

Self sealing bags may be used for marinating meats and vegetables, but are not recommended for microwaving.

Zesty Lamb Kabobs

1⅛ **cups dry red wine**
2 **tablespoons vegetable oil**
1 **cup onion,**
   finely chopped
2 **cloves garlic, crushed**
2 **tablespoons Dijon**
   mustard
1 **bay leaf**
½ **teaspoon salt**
½ **teaspoon pepper**
½ **teaspoon thyme**
¼ **teaspoon ginger**
2 **lbs. lamb, cut in 1-inch**
   cubes
2 **large green peppers,**
   cut in 1-inch squares
2 **large sweet red peppers,**
   cut in 1-inch squares
3 **medium onions,**
   cut in eighths
3 **tablespoons cornstarch**
Cooked rice

In 2-quart casserole, combine wine, oil, onion, garlic, mustard, bay leaf, salt, pepper, thyme and ginger. Add lamb cubes. Cover and marinate in refrigerator several hours or overnight. Remove lamb from marinade. Reserve marinade.

On 8-inch wooden skewers, thread red or green pepper square, onion chunk and lamb cube. Repeat, ending with onion chunk and pepper square. Place 4 kabobs on microwave-safe plate. Microwave at HIGH (10) 4 to 5 minutes. Repeat with remaining kabobs. Place kabobs on a bed of cooked rice and keep warm.

In 4-cup glass measure, combine reserved marinade and cornstarch; stir until smooth. Microwave at HIGH (10) 3 to 5 minutes until thickened, stirring every 2 minutes. Remove bay leaf. Pour sauce over kabobs before serving.

Total Microwave Cooking Time 11 to 15 Minutes
Makes 4 servings

Meat Roasting Chart for Microwave Cooking

MEAT		Power Level	Approximate Cooking Time	Internal Temperature
Beef	**Rib, Boneless Rib, Top Sirloin***			
	Rare	Medium (5)	8 to 11 min./lb.	140°F.
	Medium	Medium (5)	11 to 14 min./lb.	160°F.
	Well	Medium (5)	14 to 17 min./lb.	170°F.
	Standing Rib, high quality, bone-in roast*			
	Rare	Medium (5)	7 to 10 min./lb.	140°F.
	Medium	Medium (5)	10 to 13 min./lb.	160°F.
	Well	Medium (5)	13 to 16 min./lb.	170°F.
	Pot Roast* (2½ to 3 lbs.)			
	Chuck	Low (3)	25 to 28 min./lb.	
	Oblong glass baking dish with cooking bag			
	Rump*	Low (3)	25 to 28 min./lb.	
	3-quart casserole with lid.			
	*Turn meat over after ½ of cooking time.			
Pork	**Bone-in***	Medium (5)	12 to 15 min./lb.	170°F.
	Boneless*	Medium (5)	13 to 16 min./lb.	170°F.
	Pork Chops* (½ to 1-inch thick)			
	2 chops	Medium High (7)	15 to 18 min. total	
	4 chops	Medium High (7)	18 to 23 min. total	
	6 chops	Medium High (7)	23 to 26 min. total	
	*Turn over after ½ of cooking time.			
Ham	**Canned* (3 lbs.)**	Medium (5)	11 to 14 min./lb.	140°F.
	Butt* (3 to 4 lbs.)	Medium (5)	11 to 14 min./lb.	140°F.
	Shank* (3 to 4 lbs.)	Medium (5)	11 to 14 min./lb.	140°F.
	*Turn over after ½ of cooking time.			
Lamb	**Bone-in***			
	Medium	Medium (5)	10 to 15 min./lb.	170°F.
	Well	Medium (5)	15 to 20 min./lb.	180°F.
	Boneless*			
	Medium	Medium (5)	10 to 15 min./lb.	170°F.
	Well	Medium (5)	15 to 20 min./lb.	180°F.
	Lamb Chops* (½ to 1-inch thick)			
	2 chops	Medium High (7)	5 to 8 min. total	
	4 chops	Medium High (7)	8 to 11 min. total	
	6 chops	Medium High (7)	11 to 14 min. total	
	*Turn over after ½ of cooking time.			

Poultry

Oriental Chicken and Cashews

3 tablespoons oil
4 skinless, boneless chicken
    breasts
2 cloves garlic, minced
2 tablespoons soy sauce
1 tablespoon sherry
1 tablespoon cornstarch
¼ teaspoon ginger
1 medium green pepper,
    cut into small chunks
½ cup cashews
Cooked rice

In 2-quart oblong glass baking dish, combine oil, chicken, garlic, soy sauce, sherry, cornstarch and ginger. Microwave at HIGH (10) 3 to 4 minutes, stirring every minute. Add green pepper and cashews. Cover with plastic wrap. Microwave at HIGH (10) 2 to 3 minutes until chicken is done and green pepper is tender; stir after 1 minute. Let stand 3 minutes before serving. Serve over rice.

Total Microwave Cooking Time 5 to 7 Minutes
Makes 4 servings

Turkey with Vegetables

2 tablespoons butter
¼ lb. sliced fresh
    mushrooms
¼ cup carrots, thinly sliced
¼ cup celery, sliced
1 lb. cooked turkey,
    thinly sliced
¼ cup white wine
¼ cup chicken broth
1½ teaspoons cornstarch
¼ teaspoon salt
⅛ teaspoon pepper
1 tablespoon parsley,
    snipped

In 2-quart casserole, combine butter, mushrooms, carrots and celery. Microwave at HIGH (10) 3 to 4 minutes. Add turkey slices and Microwave at HIGH (10) 4 to 5 minutes until turkey is heated through. Combine wine, broth, cornstarch, salt, pepper and parsley; pour over turkey. Stir to coat. Microwave at HIGH (10) 2 to 3 minutes until thickened, stirring every minute.

Total Microwave Cooking Time 9 to 12 Minutes
Makes 4 servings

Sweet and Tangy Chicken

1 (2½ to 3 lb.) chicken,
    cut up
1 (8 oz.) bottle Russian
    dressing
1 cup apricot preserves
2 tablespoons mayonnaise
1 (1¾ oz.) pkg. dry onion
    soup mix

Place metal accessory rack on turntable. Preheat oven to 375°F. Arrange chicken in 2-quart oblong glass baking dish with thickest meaty pieces to outside edges. In small mixing bowl, combine salad dressing, preserves, mayonnaise and onion soup mix. Pour over chicken. Cook on Combination 40 to 45 minutes.

TO COOK BY CONVECTION: Place metal accessory rack on turntable. Preheat oven to 375°F. Convection Bake 50 to 60 minutes.

Total Combination Cooking Time 40 to 45 minutes
Total Convection Cooking Time 50 to 60 minutes
Makes 4 servings

◄ *Oriental Chicken and Cashews*

Poultry

▲ *Turkey Curry*

Turkey Curry

3 tablespoons butter
½ cup onion, chopped
1 medium apple, peeled
and coarsely chopped
¼ cup raisins
3 tablespoons all-purpose
flour
1 teaspoon curry powder
½ teaspoon coriander
¼ teaspoon cumin
¼ teaspoon ginger
1 cup half & half
1 cup hot water
1 teaspoon instant chicken
bouillon granules
3 cups cooked turkey,
chopped

In 2-quart casserole, place butter, onion, apple and raisins. Microwave at HIGH (10) 3 to 4 minutes. Add flour, curry powder, coriander, cumin and ginger; stir until smooth. Gradually stir in half & half, water and bouillon. Microwave at HIGH (10) 4 to 6 minutes, until thickened, stirring every 2 minutes. Add turkey and Microwave at HIGH (10) 1 to 2 minutes until heated through. Serve over rice.

Total Microwave Cooking Time 8 to 12 Minutes
Makes 6 servings

Roast Duck with Orange Sauce

1 (4 to 5 lb.) duck
¼ cup butter, melted
2 tablespoons cider vinegar
2 tablespoons sugar
1 cup chicken broth
2 tablespoons cornstarch
1 tablespoon orange peel, grated
½ cup orange juice
1 teaspoon lemon juice

Tuck wing tips under back of duck. Brush with melted butter. Place breast side down on trivet in 2-quart oblong glass baking dish. Set aside.

In 1½-quart casserole, combine vinegar and sugar. Microwave at HIGH (10) 2 minutes until lightly browned; stir after 1 minute. Add broth, cornstarch, orange peel, orange juice and lemon juice. Microwave at HIGH (10) 4 to 6 minutes until clear and thickened, stirring every 2 minutes. Baste duck with orange sauce. Place metal accessory rack on turntable. Preheat oven to 375°F. Cook on Combination 1 hour, basting duck every 20 minutes. Turn breast side up after 30 minutes.

Total Combination Cooking Time 1 hour
Makes 6 servings

Pierce skin of breast and legs to release fat after turning duck over.

Hot Chicken Salad

1½ cups cooked chicken, diced
½ cup celery, finely chopped
½ cup slivered almonds, toasted
½ cup butter cracker crumbs
¼ cup onion, chopped
1 (10¾ oz.) can cream of chicken soup
½ cup mayonnaise
¼ teaspoon salt
¾ cup Cheddar cheese, shredded

Place metal accessory rack on turntable. Preheat oven to 350°F. In 1½-quart casserole, combine chicken, celery, almonds, cracker crumbs, onion, chicken soup, mayonnaise and salt. Mix well. Cook on Combination 18 to 23 minutes. Sprinkle cheese over top and continue cooking 5 minutes until cheese melts.

Total Combination Cooking Time 23 to 28 Minutes
Makes 4 servings

Chicken Parmesan

½ cup seasoned dry bread crumbs
¼ cup grated Parmesan cheese
¼ teaspoon paprika
1 egg, beaten
¼ cup water
4 skinless, boneless chicken breasts, pounded thin
1 cup spaghetti sauce
1 cup mozzarella cheese, shredded

Place metal accessory rack on turntable. Preheat oven to 400°F. In small mixing bowl, combine bread crumbs, Parmesan cheese and paprika. Set aside. In shallow dish, blend egg and water together. Dip chicken in egg mixture and then in bread crumb mixture. In 2-quart oblong glass baking dish, arrange chicken. Pour spaghetti sauce over top; cover. Convection Bake 30 to 33 minutes until chicken is done. Sprinkle with cheese and continue baking 5 minutes until cheese is melted.

Total Convection Cooking Time 35 to 38 Minutes
Makes 4 servings

Pound chicken breast to ¼-inch thickness.

Poultry

Crescent-Wrapped Curried Chicken Breasts

Press crescent roll perforations together to seal.

2 cups water
4 skinless, boneless chicken
    breasts (about 1 lb.)
1 tablespoon curry powder
1 (10 oz.) pkg. frozen
    chopped spinach, thawed
    and well drained
2 tablespoons sour cream
1 (3 oz.) pkg. cream cheese,
    softened
½ teaspoon coriander
2 (8 oz.) pkgs. refrigerated
    crescent rolls
1 cup Swiss cheese,
    shredded

In 2-quart casserole, place water, chicken and curry powder. Microwave at HIGH (7) 7 to 9 minutes until chicken is done. Drain and set aside. Place metal accessory rack on turntable. Preheat oven to 400°F. In medium mixing bowl, combine spinach, sour cream, cream cheese and coriander. Divide each package of crescent rolls in half. Press perforations together to seal. On each square, place ¼ cup Swiss cheese, one chicken breast and about ¼ cup spinach mixture. Fold dough in half over chicken to form triangles; press edges to seal. Place on ungreased 12-inch pizza pan. Convection Bake 24 to 29 minutes until golden brown.

Total Convection Cooking Time 24 to 29 Minutes
Makes 4 servings

Top with chicken and ¼ cup spinach mixture.

Butter Sauce:
½ cup butter
1 tablespoon lemon juice
¼ teaspoon pepper
¼ teaspoon dry mustard
3 egg yolks, beaten

In 2-cup glass measure, place butter, lemon juice, pepper and mustard. Microwave at HIGH (10) 1 to 2 minutes until butter melts. With wire whisk, blend in egg yolks. Microwave at MEDIUM (5) 1 to 2 minutes until thickened. Pour over chicken.

Total Microwave Cooking Time 2 to 4 Minutes

Fold dough over chicken to form a triangle and seal edges.

Creamy Chicken Delight

1 cup celery, chopped
¼ cup water
3 (5 oz.) cans cooked
    chicken
1 cup rice, cooked
1 (10¾ oz.) can cream of
    chicken soup
2 tablespoons onion,
    chopped
¾ cup mayonnaise
1 (8 oz.) can sliced water
    chestnuts, drained
½ cup slivered almonds
2 teaspoons parsley flakes
½ teaspoon basil
¼ teaspoon pepper
¼ teaspoon celery seed
¼ teaspoon garlic powder
2 tablespoons butter
½ cup bread crumbs

In 4-cup glass measure, combine celery and water. Cover with plastic wrap and Microwave at HIGH (10) 2 to 3 minutes. Drain.

Place metal accessory rack on turntable. Preheat oven to 350°F. In greased 2-quart casserole, combine celery, chicken, rice, soup, onion, mayonnaise, water chestnuts, almonds, parsley flakes, basil, pepper, celery seed and garlic powder. Dot with butter and sprinkle with bread crumbs. Cook on Combination 30 to 35 minutes.

TO COOK BY CONVECTION: Place metal accessory rack on turntable. Preheat oven to 375°F. Convection Bake 35 to 40 minutes.

Total Combination Cooking Time 30 to 35 Minutes
Total Convection Cooking Time 35 to 40 Minutes
Makes 6 to 8 servings

▲ *Teriyaki Cornish Hens*

Teriyaki Cornish Hens

3 tablespoons brown sugar
2 teaspoons cornstarch
¼ teaspoon dry mustard
⅛ teaspoon ginger
½ cup teriyaki sauce
¼ cup orange juice
4 (1 to 1½ lb.) Cornish hens
1 (6 oz.) pkg. long grain
and wild rice mix,
cooked
½ cup dried apricots,
finely chopped

In 1-quart casserole, combine brown sugar, cornstarch, dry mustard and ginger. Blend in teriyaki sauce and orange juice; stir until smooth. Microwave at HIGH (10) 2 to 3 minutes until thickened, stirring every minute; set aside.

Place metal accessory rack on turntable. Preheat oven to 375°F. Remove giblets from hens; rinse with cold water and pat dry. In small mixing bowl, combine rice and apricots. Stuff hens with rice mixture and close cavities. Secure with toothpicks. In 2-quart oblong glass baking dish, place hens, breast side up, on trivet. Cook on Combination 1 hour. Brush with teriyaki sauce and continue cooking 15 to 20 minutes until done.

Total Combination Cooking Time 1 Hour 15 Minutes
to 1 Hour 20 Minutes
Makes 4 servings

Poultry

▲ *Mint-Laced Chicken*

Place fresh mint leaves in cavity of chicken.

Mint-Laced Chicken

1 (3 to 3½ lb.)
    whole chicken
½ **teaspoon salt**
¼ **teaspoon garlic powder**
¼ **teaspoon lemon pepper**
1 **cup fresh mint leaves**
¼ **cup butter, melted**
2 **tablespoons lemon juice**

Place metal accessory rack on turntable. Preheat oven to 375°F. Rinse chicken with cold water and pat dry. Combine salt, garlic powder and lemon pepper. Sprinkle inside chicken cavity. Place mint leaves in cavity of chicken.

Combine butter and lemon juice; brush over outside of chicken. Place chicken, breast side up, on trivet in 2-quart oblong glass baking dish. Cook on Combination 45 to 50 minutes until done.

Total Combination Cooking Time 45 to 50 Minutes
Makes 4 to 6 servings

Hawaiian Turkey

1 (15½ oz.) can pineapple
    chunks
1 **cup fresh snow peas**
¼ **cup water**
1 **small onion, thinly sliced**
¼ **cup green pepper,**
    chopped
1 **stalk celery, sliced**
    diagonally
2 **cups cooked turkey,**
    cubed
1 **tablespoon cornstarch**
2 **teaspoons instant chicken**
    bouillon granules
1 **tablespoon brown sugar**
3 **tablespoons soy sauce**
2 **tablespoons vinegar**

Drain pineapple, reserving juice; set aside. Place snow peas and water in 3-quart casserole. Microwave at HIGH (10) 2 to 4 minutes. Drain. Add onion, green pepper, celery, turkey and pineapple chunks.

In 4-cup glass measure, combine reserved pineapple juice, cornstarch, bouillon, brown sugar, soy sauce and vinegar. Microwave at HIGH (10) 2 to 4 minutes until sauce is clear and thickened, stirring every minute. Pour sauce over turkey and vegetables; stir to coat. Cover. Microwave at HIGH (10) 5 to 7 minutes until heated through.

Total Microwave Cooking Time 9 to 15 Minutes
Makes 4 servings

Chicken A La Roma

2 tablespoons olive oil
¾ cup green onions,
    thinly sliced
2 cloves garlic, minced
½ lb. sliced fresh
    mushrooms
1 (8 oz.) can tomato sauce
1 (6 oz.) can tomato paste
½ cup dry white wine
1 tablespoon instant
    chicken bouillon
    granules
2 teaspoons parsley flakes
1 teaspoon basil
1 teaspoon oregano
1 (2¼ oz.) can sliced ripe
    olives, drained
¼ teaspoon pepper
1 (2½ to 3 lb.) chicken,
    cut up
1 (6 oz.) jar marinated
    artichoke hearts, drained
¼ cup grated Parmesan
    cheese

In 8-inch square baking dish, place oil, onion, garlic and mushrooms. Cover with wax paper. Microwave at HIGH (10) 4 to 6 minutes. Drain.

Add tomato sauce, tomato paste, white wine, bouillon, parsley, basil, oregano, olives and pepper to mushroom mixture; blend well.

Place chicken pieces in 3-quart casserole. Add tomato mixture. Cover. Microwave at HIGH (10) 10 minutes; rearrange chicken. Microwave at MEDIUM HIGH (7) 15 to 17 minutes. Arrange artichoke hearts around chicken pieces and sprinkle with Parmesan cheese. Cover. Microwave at HIGH (10) 4 to 5 minutes. Let stand 5 minutes before serving.

TO COOK BY COMBINATION: Place metal accessory rack on turntable. Preheat oven to 375°F. Cook on Combination 45 minutes. Arrange artichoke hearts around chicken and top with Parmesan cheese. Cook on Combination 5 to 10 minutes.

Total Microwave Cooking Time 33 to 38 Minutes
Total Combination Cooking Time 50 to 55 Minutes
Makes 4 to 6 servings

Chicken Italiano

2 tablespoons olive oil
½ lb. sliced fresh
    mushrooms
½ cup onion, chopped
2 cloves garlic, minced
6 skinless, boneless chicken
    breasts
⅔ cup dry white wine
¾ teaspoon Italian herb
    seasoning
¼ teaspoon basil
1 cup spaghetti sauce
¼ cup grated Parmesan
    cheese
¼ teaspoon red pepper
    flakes

In 3-quart casserole, place oil, mushrooms, onion and garlic. Microwave at HIGH (10) 2 to 4 minutes until tender. Add chicken. Microwave at HIGH (10) 6 to 8 minutes. Turn over. Add wine, Italian seasoning and basil. Microwave at MEDIUM (5) 5 to 8 minutes.

Place metal accessory rack on turntable. Preheat oven to 350°F. Spread spaghetti sauce over chicken. Sprinkle with Parmesan cheese and red pepper flakes. Convection Bake 25 to 30 minutes.

Total Convection Cooking Time 25 to 30 Minutes
Makes 4 servings

Poultry

▲ *Chicken Cacciatore*

Chicken Cacciatore

1 (2½ to 3 lb.) chicken,
   cut up
1 medium green pepper,
   coarsely chopped
1 medium onion, sliced
1 large tomato, seeded and
   coarsely chopped
1 (15 oz.) can tomato sauce
1 (6 oz.) can tomato paste
¼ cup dry red wine
1 bay leaf
½ teaspoon oregano
¼ teaspoon fennel seed
¼ teaspoon pepper
½ cup grated Parmesan
   cheese
Capellini or spaghetti
   (optional)

In 3-quart casserole, place chicken pieces with meaty portions along outside of dish. Add green pepper and onion slices.

In 4-cup glass measure, combine tomato, tomato sauce, tomato paste, wine, bay leaf, garlic, oregano, fennel seed and pepper. Mix well and pour over chicken. Cover. Microwave at HIGH (10) 30 to 35 minutes until chicken is done and vegetables are tender. Discard bay leaf. Sprinkle with Parmesan cheese. Serve over capellini or spaghetti, if desired.

Total Microwave Cooking Time 30 to 35 Minutes
Makes 6 servings

Chicken In Pastry Shells

1 tablespoon butter
1 cup sliced fresh
    mushrooms
½ cup green pepper,
    chopped
2 tablespoons butter,
    melted
3 tablespoons all-purpose
    flour
½ cup chicken broth
½ cup milk
2 tablespoons dry sherry
½ teaspoon salt
¼ teaspoon pepper
2 (5 oz.) cans cooked
    chicken
6 pastry shells, baked

In 2-quart casserole, place 1 tablespoon butter, mushrooms and green pepper. Microwave at HIGH (10) 3 to 5 minutes until mushrooms are tender; stir after 2 minutes. Drain.

In 4-cup glass measure, combine remaining butter and flour. Gradually add broth and milk, stirring constantly until smooth. Microwave at HIGH (10) 2 to 4 minutes until thickened, stirring every minute. Add mushrooms, green pepper, sherry, salt, pepper and chicken. Microwave at HIGH (10) 5 to 7 minutes until heated through. Serve in baked pastry shells.

Total Microwave Cooking Time 10 to 16 Minutes
Makes 6 servings

Remove the center of pastry shells before filling.

Chicken Gumbo

1 (2½ to 3 lb.) chicken,
    cut up
1 lb. smoked sausage,
    cut into ¼-inch slices
2 tablespoons vegetable oil
2 cups onion, chopped
1 small green pepper,
    chopped
1 small red pepper,
    chopped
¼ cup all-purpose flour
3 cups water
2 chicken-flavored
    bouillon cubes
½ teaspoon pepper
Cooked rice

In 3-quart casserole, place chicken, sausage and oil. Microwave at HIGH (10) 10 to 12 minutes; turn chicken over after 5 minutes. In small mixing bowl, combine onion, green pepper and red pepper. Microwave at HIGH (10) 6 to 7 minutes until tender. Add to chicken.

In 4-cup glass measure, combine flour and water; stir until blended. Microwave at HIGH (10) 3 to 5 minutes; stir after 2 minutes. Add bouillon and pepper; mix well and pour over chicken and vegetables. Place metal accessory rack on turntable. Preheat oven to 350°F. Cook on Combination 35 to 40 minutes. Serve over rice.

Total Combination Cooking Time 35 to 40 Minutes
Makes 4 to 6 servings

Curried Chicken and Rice

2 tablespoons butter
6 skinless, boneless chicken
    breasts, cut into ½-inch
    cubes
1 medium onion, chopped
2 (10¾ oz.) cans cream of
    chicken soup
¼ cup fresh parsley,
    snipped
1 tablespoon curry powder
¼ teaspoon seasoned salt
3 cups cooked rice

In 3-quart casserole, place butter, chicken and onion. Microwave at HIGH (10) 7 to 8 minutes until chicken is no longer pink, stirring every 2 minutes. Add chicken soup, parsley, curry powder, seasoned salt and rice. Place metal accessory rack on turntable. Preheat oven to 350°F. Convection Bake 25 to 30 minutes.

Total Convection Cooking Time 25 to 30 Minutes
Makes 6 servings

Poultry

Chicken Normandy

3 tablespoons butter
2 large apples, sliced
   (2 cups)
1 cup celery, sliced
3 tablespoons cornstarch
¼ cup apple juice
½ cup sweet and sour sauce
1 cup chicken broth
¼ cup whipping cream
2 tablespoons apple brandy
½ teaspoon salt
¼ teaspoon white pepper
8 skinless, boneless chicken
   breasts

In 2-quart oblong glass baking dish, place butter, apples and celery. Microwave at HIGH (10) 4 minutes. In medium mixing bowl, combine cornstarch, apple juice, sweet and sour sauce, chicken broth, whipping cream and apple brandy. Pour over apples. Microwave at HIGH (10) 4 to 6 minutes until slightly thickened, stirring every 3 minutes. Add salt and pepper. Arrange chicken breasts over apples. Cover with vented plastic wrap. Microwave at HIGH (10) 10 to 14 minutes until chicken is thoroughly cooked.

Total Microwave Cooking Time 18 to 24 Minutes
Makes 8 servings

Chicken & Peppers in White Wine Sauce

½ lb. bacon, cut up
1 (3 lb.) chicken, cut up
1 large onion, coarsely
   chopped
1 large green pepper,
   coarsely chopped
1 large red pepper,
   coarsely chopped
¼ teaspoon ground thyme
¼ teaspoon salt
¼ teaspoon pepper
1 (2¼ oz.) can sliced ripe
   olives, drained
1 cup dry white wine

In 3-quart casserole, place bacon and Microwave at HIGH (10) 7 to 9 minutes until crisp. Drain, reserving 3 tablespoons drippings. Place chicken in casserole, skin side down; add reserved bacon drippings. Microwave at HIGH (10) 8 minutes; turn chicken over after 4 minutes and drain off fat. Add onion, green pepper, red pepper, thyme, salt, pepper and olives. Pour wine over chicken and vegetables; cover. Microwave at HIGH (10) 20 to 23 minutes until done.

Total Microwave Cooking Time 28 to 31 Minutes
Makes 6 servings

Rice and Chicken Livers

Prick livers with toothpick prior to cooking to prevent bursting.

1 cup long grain rice
2⅓ cups chicken broth
½ teaspoon seasoned salt
3 tablespoons fresh
   parsley, snipped
2 stalks celery, chopped
¼ teaspoon thyme
½ cup butter
½ cup onion, chopped
½ lb. sliced fresh
   mushrooms
1 lb. chicken livers
¼ cup grated Parmesan
   cheese

In 2-quart casserole, combine rice, chicken broth, seasoned salt, parsley, celery and thyme. Micro-wave at HIGH (10) 15 minutes; stir. Microwave at MEDIUM HIGH (7) 10 to 15 minutes until rice is tender. Discard bay leaf.

In 3-quart casserole, combine butter, onion and mush-rooms. Microwave at HIGH (10) 6 to 8 minutes; stir after 3 minutes. Prick chicken livers with toothpick. Add chicken livers to mushroom mixture and Microwave at HIGH (10) 8 to 10 minutes, stirring every 3 minutes. Add rice mixture; stir well. Sprinkle with Parmesan cheese. Place metal accessory rack on turntable. Preheat oven to 350°F. Convection Bake 25 to 30 minutes.

Total Convection Cooking Time 25 to 30 Minutes
Makes 4 to 6 servings

▲ *Chicken with Spicy Cheddar Sauce*

Chicken with Spicy Cheddar Sauce

½ **cup cornflake crumbs**
½ **teaspoon paprika**
¼ **teaspoon garlic powder**
4 **skinless, boneless chicken breasts**
½ **cup cheese spread with jalapeño peppers**
¼ **cup pitted ripe olives, sliced**
1 **(2 oz.) jar sliced pimento, drained**

In medium mixing bowl, combine cornflake crumbs, paprika and garlic powder. Rinse chicken in water, then coat with crumb mixture. In 2-quart oblong glass baking dish, arrange chicken with meaty portions toward the edges of the dish. Cover loosely with plastic wrap. Microwave at HIGH (10) 12 to 14 minutes until thoroughly cooked. Transfer chicken to platter and keep warm.

In 2-cup glass measure, combine cheese spread, olives and pimento. Microwave at HIGH (10) 1 minute until heated through. Pour sauce over chicken.

Total Microwave Cooking Time 13 to 15 Minutes
Makes 4 servings

Sauteed Chicken Livers with Wine Sauce

2 **tablespoons onion, minced**
2 **cloves garlic, minced**
3 **tablespoons butter**
2 **tablespoons all-purpose flour**
1 **cup beef broth**
3 **tablespoons dry red wine**
¼ **cup all-purpose flour**
½ **teaspoon garlic salt**
1 **lb. chicken livers**
2 **tablespoons butter, melted**
1 **(6 oz.) pkg. long grain and wild rice, cooked**

In 1½-quart casserole, combine onions, garlic and butter. Microwave at HIGH (10) 2 to 3 minutes until onions are transparent. Add 2 tablespoons flour; stir until smooth. Gradually add beef broth. Microwave at HIGH (10) 2 to 3 minutes until thickened, stirring every minute. Blend in wine, set aside.

Combine remaining flour and garlic salt. Coat chicken livers with flour mixture. Prick chicken livers to prevent bursting. In 2-quart casserole, place 2 tablespoons melted butter and chicken livers. Microwave at HIGH (10) 6 to 8 minutes; turn livers every 2 minutes. Pour wine sauce over chicken livers. Microwave at HIGH (10) 3 to 4 minutes until heated. Serve over rice.

Total Microwave Cooking Time 13 to 18 Minutes
Makes 4 servings

Poultry

Turkey Tetrazzini

¼ cup butter, melted
¼ cup all-purpose flour
1 cup chicken broth
1 cup half & half
4 cups cooked turkey, cut up
1 (2 oz.) jar sliced pimento, drained
1 (7 oz.) pkg. spaghetti, cooked and drained
1 (4 oz.) can sliced mushrooms, drained
½ teaspoon salt
½ teaspoon pepper
¼ cup grated Parmesan cheese

In 3-quart casserole, combine butter and flour. Gradually add broth and half & half, stirring until smooth. Microwave at MEDIUM HIGH (7) 5 to 6 minutes until thickened, stirring every 2 minutes. Add turkey, pimento, spaghetti, mushrooms, salt and pepper. Sprinkle Parmesan cheese over top. Place metal accessory rack on turntable. Preheat oven to 350°F. Cook on Combination 23 to 28 minutes.

Total Combination Cooking Time 23 to 28 Minutes
Makes 6 servings

Chicken and Vegetables

½ cup all-purpose flour
½ teaspoon seasoned salt
¼ teaspoon pepper
¼ teaspoon cumin
1 (3 lb.) chicken, cut up
3 tablespoons olive oil
1 small green pepper, thinly sliced
1 small red pepper, thinly sliced
2 cloves garlic, minced
3 medium tomatoes, chopped
1 cup sliced fresh mushrooms
1 medium zucchini, thinly sliced
1½ cups hot water
Cooked rice

In a plastic bag, combine flour, seasoned salt, pepper and cumin. Add chicken pieces and shake to coat. In 3-quart casserole, place chicken and vegetable oil. Microwave at HIGH (10) 6 to 7 minutes. Remove chicken from casserole and set aside. Add green pepper, red pepper and garlic. Microwave at HIGH (10) 5 to 6 minutes until tender; stir after 3 minutes. Add tomatoes, mushrooms, zucchini and water. Return chicken pieces to casserole. Place metal accessory rack on turntable. Preheat oven to 350°F. Convection Bake 40 to 45 minutes until chicken is tender. Serve over rice.

Total Convection Cooking Time 40 to 45 Minutes
Makes 6 servings

Baked Chicken Bites

Place coated chicken pieces on pizza pan.

1 cup bread crumbs
½ cup grated Parmesan cheese
½ teaspoon lemon pepper
½ teaspoon salt
½ teaspoon thyme
¼ teaspoon garlic powder
¾ cup butter, melted
6 skinless, boneless chicken breasts, cut into 1½-inch cubes

Place metal accessory rack on turntable. Preheat oven to 400°F. In shallow dish, combine bread crumbs, Parmesan cheese, lemon pepper, salt, thyme and garlic powder. Mix well. Dip chicken pieces in butter and coat with bread crumb mixture. Place coated chicken pieces on 12-inch pizza pan. Convection Bake 25 to 30 minutes until chicken is golden brown.

Total Convection Cooking Time 25 to 30 Minutes
Makes 6 servings

Hot Brown

3 tablespoons butter,
   melted
¼ cup all-purpose flour
1½ cups milk
¼ teaspoon salt
¼ teaspoon white pepper
¾ cup sharp Cheddar
   cheese, shredded
6 slices bread, toasted
¾ lb. turkey, thinly sliced
12 bacon strips, cooked
6 slices tomato
¼ cup grated Parmesan
   cheese

In 4-cup glass measure, combine butter and flour. Stir until smooth. Gradually add milk, salt, pepper and cheese. Microwave at HIGH (10) 3 to 5 minutes until thickened and cheese is melted, stirring every minute.

Place metal accessory rack on turntable. Preheat oven to 400°F. Place toast on 12-inch pizza pan. Arrange turkey slices on toast and cover with cheese sauce. Convection Bake 12 to 15 minutes until heated through. Top with bacon strips and tomato slices. Sprinkle with Parmesan cheese.

Total Convection Cooking Time 12 to 15 Minutes
Makes 6 servings

Spicy Marinated Chicken

2 cloves garlic, crushed
3 tablespoons lemon juice
½ teaspoon ginger
½ teaspoon nutmeg
½ teaspoon cinnamon
½ teaspoon coriander
½ teaspoon paprika
¼ teaspoon turmeric
⅛ teaspoon cayenne pepper
4 skinless, boneless chicken
   breasts
½ cup sour cream

Combine garlic, lemon juice, ginger, nutmeg, cinnamon, coriander, paprika, turmeric and cayenne pepper. Place chicken breasts in 8-inch square baking dish. Spread marinade over chicken. Cover with plastic wrap and marinate in refrigerator several hours or overnight. Remove dish from refrigerator; vent plastic wrap. Microwave at HIGH (10) 13 to 18 minutes; turn chicken over after 7 minutes. Top with sour cream.

Total Microwave Cooking Time 13 to 18 Minutes
Makes 4 servings

Chicken Stroganoff

3 tablespoons butter,
   melted, divided
¼ teaspoon salt
¼ teaspoon pepper
6 skinless, boneless chicken
   breasts cut into 1-inch
   strips
1 medium onion, sliced
1 cup sliced fresh
   mushrooms
2 medium zucchini, sliced
1 tablespoon all-purpose
   flour
1 cup chicken broth
½ teaspoon basil
1 (8 oz.) carton sour cream
2 teaspoons dry mustard
Cooked rice or noodles

In 2-quart casserole, place 2 tablespoons butter, salt and pepper. Coat chicken pieces in butter. Microwave at HIGH (10) 8 to 9 minutes; stir after 4 minutes. Add onion, mushrooms and zucchini. Microwave at HIGH (10) 4 to 6 minutes; stir after 2 minutes.

In 4-cup glass measure, combine 1 tablespoon melted butter and flour. Add chicken broth and basil; stir well. Microwave at HIGH (10) 3 to 5 minutes, stirring every minute. Add sour cream and mustard; stir to blend. Pour over chicken and vegetables. Microwave at HIGH (10) 3 to 5 minutes until heated through. Serve over rice or noodles.

Total Microwave Cooking Time 18 to 25 Minutes
Makes 4 to 6 servings

Fish & Seafood

Baked Lobster Tails

4 lobster tails, thawed
 (about 8 oz. ea.)
3 tablespoons butter,
 melted
⅓ cup seasoned dry bread
 crumbs
⅛ teaspoon onion powder
⅛ teaspoon paprika
⅛ teaspoon salt

With kitchen shears, cut lobster through center of soft shell (underneath) to the tail. Lift lobster out of shell by loosening with fingers, leaving meat attached to tail section. (Lobster meat will rest on shell.) Arrange in 10-inch glass pie plate, tails toward center. In small mixing bowl, combine butter, bread crumbs, onion powder, paprika and salt; sprinkle over lobster. Cover with wax paper. Microwave at MEDIUM HIGH (7) 10 to 13 minutes until lobster is done. Let stand 5 minutes. Serve with Lemon Butter, if desired.

Lemon Butter: In small bowl, Microwave ½ cup butter and 2 tablespoons lemon juice at MEDIUM (5) 1 to 2 minutes until butter is melted.

Total Microwave Cooking Time 10 to 13 Minutes
Makes 4 servings

Scalloped Oysters

2 tablespoons butter
½ cup onion, chopped
½ cup green pepper,
 chopped
¼ cup butter, melted
2 cups buttery cracker
 crumbs
½ teaspoon salt
⅛ teaspoon pepper
2 (8 oz.) cans fresh oysters,
 drained
1 teaspoon Worcestershire
 sauce
1 cup evaporated milk

In 1-quart casserole, place butter, onion and green pepper. Microwave at HIGH (10) 2 to 3 minutes until tender. Set aside. In small mixing bowl, combine butter, cracker crumbs, salt and pepper. Mix well.

In 2-quart casserole, place ⅓ of crumb mixture, one can of oysters and half of onion-green pepper mixture. Repeat layers ending with cracker crumbs.

In small mixing bowl, combine Worcestershire sauce and evaporated milk; pour over layered casserole. Place metal accessory rack on turntable. Preheat oven to 350°F. Convection Bake 30 to 35 minutes.

Total Convection Cooking Time 30 to 35 Minutes
Makes 6 servings

Salmon Loaf

2 (16 oz.) cans salmon,
 drained with bone and
 skin removed
¾ cup dry bread crumbs
½ cup milk
1 egg, beaten
¼ cup butter, melted
2 tablespoons grated
 Parmesan cheese
½ teaspoon salt
¼ teaspoon white pepper

In large mixing bowl, combine salmon, bread crumbs, milk, egg, butter, Parmesan cheese, salt and pepper. Mix well. Pack mixture firmly into 8x4x3-inch glass loaf dish. Microwave at MEDIUM HIGH (7) 12 to 16 minutes.

TO COOK BY COMBINATION: Place metal accessory rack on turntable. Preheat oven to 350°F. Cook on Combination 22 to 26 minutes.

Total Microwave Cooking Time 12 to 16 Minutes
Total Combination Cooking Time 22 to 26 Minutes
Makes 4 to 6 servings

Fish & Seafood

▲ *Salmon Steaks*

Sprinkle lemon pepper onto buttered dish for extra flavor.

Salmon Steaks

1 tablespoon butter
2 teaspoons lemon pepper
6 (5 oz.) salmon steaks
2 teaspoons lemon juice
1 teaspoon lemon pepper
½ teaspoon garlic powder
½ teaspoon onion powder
6 thin onion slices
3 lemon slices, halved
1 teaspoon tarragon
½ teaspoon paprika
Dash salt

Place butter in 2-quart oblong glass baking dish. Microwave at HIGH (10) 1 to 1½ minutes until melted. Coat bottom of dish with butter and sprinkle with lemon pepper. Place salmon steaks in prepared dish. Sprinkle with lemon juice, lemon pepper, garlic powder and onion powder. Place one onion slice and one lemon slice on each salmon steak. Sprinkle with tarragon, paprika and salt. Place metal accessory rack on turntable. Preheat oven to 350°F. Cook on Combination 18 to 21 minutes.

Total Combination Cooking Time 18 to 21 Minutes
Makes 6 servings

Shrimp with Dill Sauce

2 tablespoons onion, chopped
1 tablespoon butter
1½ lbs. medium shrimp, peeled and deveined
½ cup white wine
3 tablespoons butter, melted
3 tablespoons all-purpose flour
1 cup milk
3 tablespoons lemon juice
½ teaspoon garlic salt
1 teaspoon dillweed
Cooked rice

In 2-quart casserole, place onion and 1 tablespoon butter. Microwave at HIGH (10) 1 to 2 minutes until onion is tender. Add shrimp and wine. Microwave at HIGH (10) 5 to 7 minutes, stirring every 2 minutes.

In medium bowl, combine melted butter and flour, stirring until smooth. Gradually add milk, stirring constantly. Microwave at MEDIUM HIGH (7) 4 to 6 minutes, stirring every 2 minutes. Add lemon juice, garlic salt and dillweed. Pour over shrimp mixture. Mix well. Microwave at HIGH (10) 6 to 8 minutes, stirring every 3 minutes. Serve over rice.

Total Microwave Cooking Time 16 to 23 Minutes
Makes 4 to 6 servings

Fish Amandine

½ cup slivered almonds
¼ cup butter
1 lb. thin fish fillets
1 teaspoon fresh parsley, snipped
¼ teaspoon salt
¼ teaspoon lemon pepper
¼ teaspoon dillweed

In 8-inch square baking dish, place almonds and butter. Microwave at HIGH (10) 5 to 6 minutes until almonds are golden brown. Remove almonds and set aside. Place fish in baking dish, turning to coat both sides. Sprinkle with parsley, salt, lemon pepper, dillweed and almonds. Cover with wax paper. Microwave at HIGH (10) 4 to 6 minutes until fish flakes easily when tested with a fork. Let stand 1 minute before serving.

TO COOK BY COMBINATION: Place metal accessory rack on turntable. Preheat oven to 350°F. Cook, uncovered, on Combination 11 to 14 minutes.

TO COOK BY CONVECTION: Place metal accessory rack on turntable. Preheat oven to 350°F. Convection Bake, uncovered, 14 to 18 minutes.

Total Microwave Cooking Time 9 to 12 Minutes
Total Combination Cooking Time 11 to 14 Minutes
Total Convection Cooking Time 14 to 18 Minutes
Makes 2 servings

Shrimp Enchiladas

¾ cup onion, chopped, divided
¼ cup green pepper, chopped
¼ cup red pepper, chopped
1 tablespoon butter
2 tablespoons all-purpose flour
½ cup whipping cream
¼ teaspoon garlic powder
¼ teaspoon oregano
¼ teaspoon salt
⅛ teaspoon pepper
1½ cups Monterey Jack cheese, shredded, divided
½ cup sour cream
½ lb. cooked shrimp, chopped
1 cup tomato, chopped, divided
8 (6-inch) flour tortillas

In 1½-quart casserole, place ½ cup onion, green pepper, red pepper and butter. Microwave at HIGH (10) 3 to 4 minutes, stirring after 2 minutes. Add flour; stir until smooth. Stir in cream, garlic powder, oregano, salt and pepper. Microwave at HIGH (10) 2 to 4 minutes, stirring after 1 minute. Add ¾ cup cheese; stir until melted. Add sour cream; blend well.

In small bowl, combine half of cream sauce, shrimp and ½ cup tomato. Spoon 2 tablespoons mixture into each tortilla; roll up tightly. Arrange seam side down in 2-quart oblong glass baking dish. Spoon remaining cream sauce over tortillas. Place metal accessory rack on turntable. Preheat oven to 350°F. Convection Bake 25 to 30 minutes. Sprinkle enchiladas with remaining ¾ cup cheese, ½ cup tomato and ¼ cup onion.

Total Convection Cooking Time 25 to 30 Minutes
Makes 4 servings

Fish & Seafood

▲ *Creamy Crabmeat*
and Almonds

Creamy Crabmeat and Almonds

½ cup sliced fresh
   mushrooms
1 small green pepper, cut in
   thin strips
2 tablespoons butter
2 (6 oz.) cans crabmeat,
   drained and flaked
⅓ cup slivered almonds
1 tablespoon orange juice
1 teaspoon lemon juice
2 (10½ oz.) cans cream of
   celery soup
⅓ cup ripe olives, quartered
1 (4 oz.) jar sliced pimento,
   drained
2 tablespoons fresh parsley,
   snipped
¼ teaspoon hot sauce
Cooked rice

In 3-quart casserole, combine mushrooms, green pepper and butter. Microwave at HIGH (10) 2 to 3 minutes until mushrooms are tender. Add crabmeat, almonds, orange juice, lemon juice, celery soup, olives, pimento, parsley and hot sauce. Cover with wax paper. Microwave at HIGH (10) 8 to 10 minutes until hot; stir after 6 minutes. Let stand, covered, 5 minutes. Serve over rice.

Total Microwave Cooking Time 10 to 13 Minutes
Makes 6 to 8 servings

Tuna Croquettes with Lemon Sauce

1 cup dry bread crumbs
1 (6 oz.) can water-packed
    tuna, drained
1 cup carrots, grated
½ cup milk
½ cup celery, diced
1 egg, beaten
1 tablespoon onion, minced
½ teaspoon salt
¼ teaspoon pepper

Lemon Sauce:
1 cup milk, divided
1 tablespoon cornstarch
2 tablespoons butter,
    melted
⅛ teaspoon pepper
⅓ cup fresh parsley,
    snipped
1½ tablespoons lemon juice

Place metal accessory rack on turntable. Preheat oven to 375°F.

In large mixing bowl, combine dry bread crumbs, tuna, carrots, milk, celery, egg, onion, salt and pepper. Mix well. Shape into 6 cone-shaped portions. Place on greased 12-inch pizza pan. Convection Bake 18 to 20 minutes. Serve with Lemon Sauce.

Total Convection Cooking Time 18 to 20 Minutes
Makes 4 to 6 servings

In small mixing bowl, combine ¼ cup milk and cornstarch; stir until smooth. Add remaining ¾ cup milk, butter and pepper. Microwave at HIGH (10) 3 to 4 minutes; stir after 2 minutes. Stir in parsley and lemon juice.

Total Microwave Cooking Time 3 to 4 Minutes
Makes 1 cup

Shape tuna mixture into 6 cone-shaped portions.

Shrimp Pilaf

¼ cup butter
½ cup onion, thinly sliced
⅓ cup green pepper, diced
2 cups instant rice
2 cups hot water
2 (8 oz.) cans tomato sauce
1 teaspoon seasoned salt
¼ teaspoon pepper
¼ teaspoon dry mustard
1½ cups canned shrimp

In 2-quart casserole, place butter, onion and green pepper. Microwave at HIGH (10) 3 to 4 minutes; stir after 2 minutes. Add rice, water, tomato sauce, seasoned salt, pepper, mustard and shrimp. Mix well. Microwave at HIGH (10) 8 to 10 minutes, stirring every 3 minutes.

Total Microwave Cooking Time 11 to 14 Minutes
Makes 6 servings

Scallops In Wine Sauce

½ cup hot water
¾ lb. scallops
3 tablespoons butter
½ teaspoon garlic powder
2 green onions, chopped
¼ teaspoon paprika
2 tablespoons dry white
    wine
1 tablespoon lemon juice

In 2-quart casserole, place water and scallops. Cover. Microwave at HIGH (10) 3 to 5 minutes until scallops are opaque; stir after 2 minutes. Drain and set aside.

In 2-cup glass measure, combine butter, garlic powder, onions, paprika, wine and lemon juice. Microwave at HIGH (10) 2 to 4 minutes. Pour over scallops.

Total Microwave Cooking Time 5 to 9 Minutes
Makes 2 to 3 servings

Fish & Seafood

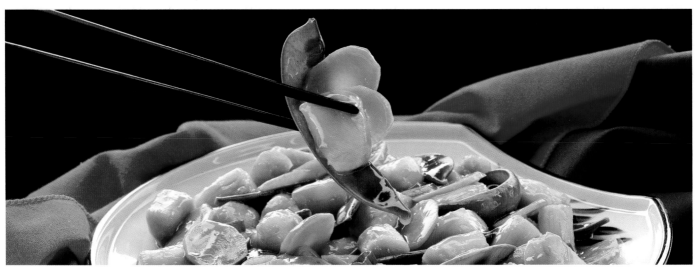

▲ *Scallops Oriental*

Scallops Oriental

1 lb. scallops
½ cup water
1½ cups carrots, thinly
    sliced
2 tablespoons green onion,
    sliced
¼ teaspoon garlic powder
1 tablespoon vegetable oil
1 tablespoon cornstarch
¾ teaspoon sugar
½ teaspoon ginger
½ cup chicken broth
2 tablespoons soy sauce
2 tablespoons dry sherry
1 (6 oz.) pkg. frozen snow
    peas, thawed

In 2-quart casserole, place scallops and water. Cover. Microwave at HIGH (10) 4 to 6 minutes until scallops are opaque, stirring every 2 minutes. Drain and set aside.

In 2-quart casserole, combine carrots, green onion, garlic powder and oil. Cover. Microwave at HIGH (10) 3 to 4 minutes until vegetables are crisp-tender. Stir in cornstarch, sugar, ginger, chicken broth, soy sauce and sherry. Microwave at HIGH (10) 2 to 3 minutes until thickened, stirring every minute. Add snow peas. Microwave at HIGH (10) 2 to 3 minutes until snow peas are crisp-tender, stirring every minute. Add scallops. Microwave at HIGH (10) 1 to 2 minutes until heated through.

Total Microwave Cooking Time 12 to 18 Minutes
Makes 4 to 6 servings

Baked Fish with Cheese

1 lb. fish fillets
1 tablespoon tarragon
½ teaspoon seasoned salt
2 tablespoons butter
¼ cup sour cream
1 cup mozzarella cheese,
    shredded

Arrange fish in 2-quart oblong glass baking dish. Sprinkle with tarragon and seasoned salt. Dot with butter; cover with wax paper. Microwave at HIGH (10) 2 to 3 minutes. Combine sour cream and cheese; spread on fish. Cover with wax paper and Microwave at HIGH (10) 2 to 3 minutes until fish flakes easily when tested with a fork.

TO COOK BY CONVECTION: Place metal accessory rack on turntable. Preheat oven to 350°F. Convection Bake 10 to 15 minutes. Top with cheese mixture and continue cooking 5 to 10 minutes longer.

Total Microwave Cooking Time 4 to 6 Minutes
Total Convection Cooking Time 15 to 25 Minutes
Makes 3 to 4 servings

Baked Scrod

2 tablespoons olive oil
1 medium onion, thinly
    sliced
2 cups fresh mushrooms,
    thinly sliced
2 teaspoons oregano
1 teaspoon thyme
½ teaspoon garlic powder
¼ teaspoon salt
¼ teaspoon lemon pepper
2 tablespoons vegetable oil
2 lbs. scrod, cut into 4 equal
    portions
2 tablespoons fresh parsley,
    snipped

In 2-quart casserole, combine olive oil, onion, mushrooms, oregano, thyme, garlic powder, salt and lemon pepper. Microwave at HIGH (10) 4 to 5 minutes until onion is transparent and mushrooms are tender.

Place metal accessory rack on turntable. Preheat oven to 450°F. Cut aluminum foil into 4 (12 x 12-inch) pieces. Brush foil with oil and place fish portions on the foil. Divide filling evenly over fish. Sprinkle with parsley. Fold foil, crimping edges to seal. Place foil packets on 12-inch pizza pan. Convection Bake 15 to 20 minutes.

Total Convection Cooking Time 15 to 20 Minutes
Makes 4 servings

Place fish on foil and spoon ¼ of vegetable filling over each portion.

Seafood Marinara

2 tablespoons butter,
    melted
¼ teaspoon garlic powder
2 tomatoes, peeled and
    chopped
1 tablespoon tomato paste
¼ cup white wine
2 teaspoons fresh parsley,
    snipped
¾ teaspoon basil
¼ teaspoon lemon pepper
½ lb. scallops
½ lb. shrimp, peeled and
    deveined

In 1-quart casserole, combine butter, garlic powder, tomatoes, tomato paste, wine, parsley, basil and lemon pepper. Microwave at HIGH (10) 3 to 4 minutes; stir after 2 minutes. Puree tomato mixture in electric blender at high speed for 1 minute.

In 2-quart casserole, place scallops and shrimp. Add tomato mixture. Microwave at HIGH (10) 5 to 7 minutes. Let stand 5 minutes. Serve over pasta.

Total Microwave Cooking Time 8 to 11 Minutes
Makes 4 servings

Completely enclose fish in foil, and crimp edges to seal.

Italian Haddock

2 tablespoons olive oil
1 tablespoon lemon juice
1 cup tomatoes, chopped
1½ cups sliced fresh
    mushrooms
¼ cup onion, chopped
¼ cup green pepper,
    chopped
2 tablespoons fresh parsley,
    snipped
¾ teaspoon oregano
½ teaspoon seasoned salt
¼ teaspoon garlic powder
1 (16 oz.) pkg. frozen
    haddock fillets, thawed

In 2-quart casserole, combine olive oil, lemon juice, tomatoes, mushrooms, onion, green pepper, parsley, oregano, seasoned salt and garlic powder. Cover. Microwave at HIGH (10) 3 to 5 minutes until onion is tender; stir after 2 minutes.

Place fish in 2-quart oblong glass baking dish. Spoon vegetable mixture over fillets. Cover with vented plastic wrap. Microwave at HIGH (10) 2 to 4 minutes until fish flakes easily when tested with a fork. Let stand 5 minutes.

Total Microwave Cooking Time 5 to 9 Minutes
Makes 4 to 6 servings

Chicken Pot Pie

½ cup onion, chopped
½ cup celery, chopped
3 tablespoons vegetable oil
⅛ cup all-purpose flour
2 cups chicken broth
3 cups cooked chicken, chopped
1 (10 oz.) pkg. frozen peas and carrots, thawed
1 (8 oz.) can whole kernel corn, drained
1 (2 oz.) jar sliced pimento, drained
½ teaspoon thyme
½ teaspoon salt
¼ teaspoon white pepper
Pastry for 2-crust (9-inch) pie
Milk (optional)

In 2-quart casserole, place onion, celery and oil. Microwave at HIGH (10) 2 to 3 minutes until vegetables are crisp-tender. Add flour, stirring until smooth. Add chicken broth. Microwave at HIGH (10) 5 to 6 minutes until thickened, stirring every 2 minutes. Add chicken, peas and carrots, corn, pimento, thyme, salt and pepper. Spoon filling evenly into an 11x7x2-inch glass baking dish. Top with pastry, crimping edges of pastry around inside of dish. Use any leftover pastry to make decorative cut-outs for the top of pie, if desired. Vent crust to allow steam to escape. Brush pastry lightly with milk, if desired. Place metal accessory rack on turntable. Preheat oven to 400°F. Cook on Combination 30 to 35 minutes until golden brown.

Total Combination Cooking Time 30 to 35 Minutes
Makes 6 servings

Lasagna

1 lb. ground beef
½ cup onion, chopped
1 (26 oz.) jar spaghetti sauce
1 (15 oz.) carton ricotta cheese
1 egg, beaten
½ teaspoon oregano
½ teaspoon basil
¼ teaspoon garlic powder
¼ teaspoon seasoned salt
6 no-boil lasagna noodles
1 (12 oz.) pkg. shredded mozzarella cheese, divided
½ cup grated Parmesan cheese

In 2-quart casserole, place beef and onion. Cover. Microwave at HIGH (10) 5 to 7 minutes until beef is thoroughly cooked; stir after 3 minutes. Drain. Stir in spaghetti sauce. Set aside.

In small mixing bowl, combine ricotta cheese, egg, oregano, basil, garlic powder and seasoned salt.

In 2-quart oblong glass baking dish, spread ⅛ of meat sauce over bottom. Top with half of lasagna noodles, half of cheese mixture and half of mozzarella cheese. Repeat layers, ending with meat sauce; cover. Place metal accessory rack on turntable. Preheat oven to 375°F. Cook on Combination 25 minutes. Uncover, sprinkle with Parmesan cheese and continue cooking on Combination 8 to 10 minutes. Let stand 10 minutes.

TO COOK BY CONVECTION: Place metal accessory rack on turntable. Preheat oven to 350°F. Bake 30 minutes. Uncover; sprinkle with Parmesan cheese and continue baking 8 to 10 minutes.

Total Combination Cooking Time 33 to 35 Minutes
Total Convection Cooking Time 38 to 40 Minutes
Makes 4 to 6 servings

Casseroles

▲ *Vegetable Lasagna*

Wear gloves when chopping hot peppers to protect from burning reaction.

Noodles Con Carne

½ lb. ground beef
½ lb. hot bulk sausage
½ cup green pepper, chopped
¼ cup onion, chopped
½ teaspoon salt
⅛ teaspoon pepper
1 hot pepper, chopped (optional)
1 (15 oz.) can chili beans
1 tablespoon chili powder
1 (8 oz.) can tomato sauce
2 cups Cheddar cheese, shredded
1 (8 oz.) pkg. wide egg noodles, cooked and drained

In 2½-quart casserole, crumble ground beef, sausage, green pepper, onion, salt, pepper and hot pepper. Cover and microwave at HIGH (10) 6 to 8 minutes until meat is browned and onion is tender, stirring every 3 minutes. Drain. Add chili beans, chili powder, tomato sauce, Cheddar cheese and egg noodles, mixing well. Cover and microwave at HIGH (10) 15 to 20 minutes until bubbly.

TO COOK BY COMBINATION: Place metal accessory rack on turntable. Preheat oven to 350°F. Cover. Cook on Combination 26 to 31 minutes until bubbly.

Total Microwave Cooking Time 21 to 28 Minutes
Total Combination Cooking Time 26 to 31 Minutes
Makes 12 servings

Vegetable Lasagna

1 cup onion, chopped
1 cup carrots, shredded
1 cup fresh mushrooms,
  coarsely chopped
2 cups small curd
  cottage cheese
2 eggs, beaten
¼ cup grated Parmesan
  cheese
1 teaspoon oregano
1 (14 oz.) jar spaghetti
  sauce, divided
6 no-boil lasagna noodles
1 (10 oz.) pkg. frozen
  chopped spinach, thawed
  and well drained
1 large tomato, coarsely
  chopped
1½ cups mozzarella cheese,
  shredded

In 1½-quart casserole, combine onion, carrots and mushrooms; cover. Microwave at HIGH (10) 5 to 7 minutes until vegetables are tender. Drain and set aside. In small mixing bowl, combine cottage cheese, eggs, Parmesan cheese and oregano.

In 2-quart oblong glass baking dish, layer half of spaghetti sauce, 3 lasagna noodles, all onion-carrot-mushroom mixture and half of cheese mixture.

Cover with remaining noodles, spaghetti sauce, spinach and cheese mixture. Top with tomatoes and mozzarella cheese; cover. Microwave at HIGH (10) 22 to 26 minutes. Let stand 10 minutes.

TO COOK BY COMBINATION: Place metal accessory rack on turntable. Preheat oven to 350°F. Cook on Combination 30 to 35 minutes.

TO COOK BY CONVECTION: Place metal accessory rack on turntable. Preheat oven to 350°F. Convection Bake 40 to 45 minutes.

Total Microwave Cooking Time 27 to 33 Minutes
Total Combination Cooking Time 32 to 37 Minutes
Total Convection Cooking Time 40 to 45 Minutes
Makes 6 servings

Spread half of cheese mixture over mixed vegetables to form first layer.

Form the second layer with remaining ingredients, starting with the noodles.

Italian Beef and Rice Casserole

1 lb. ground beef
1 cup onion, chopped
½ cup green pepper,
  chopped
½ cup celery, chopped
1 (14½ oz.) can tomatoes
1 (6 oz.) can Italian tomato
  paste
1 (4 oz.) can mushroom
  pieces, drained
1 cup rice, cooked
2 tablespoons fresh
  parsley, snipped
½ teaspoon salt
¼ teaspoon thyme
¼ teaspoon pepper
¼ teaspoon marjoram
1 cup Cheddar cheese,
  shredded

In 2-quart casserole, combine ground beef, onion, green pepper and celery. Microwave at HIGH (10) 5 to 7 minutes until vegetables are tender. Drain. Add tomatoes, tomato paste, mushrooms, rice, parsley, salt, thyme, pepper and marjoram. Microwave at HIGH (10) 15 to 18 minutes. Top with Cheddar cheese and continue to Microwave at HIGH (10) 2 to 3 minutes.

TO COOK BY COMBINATION: Place metal accessory rack on turntable. Preheat oven to 350°F. Cook on Combination 23 to 28 minutes. Top with Cheddar cheese and continue cooking 5 minutes.

TO COOK BY CONVECTION: Place metal accessory rack on turntable. Preheat oven to 350°F. Convection Bake 35 to 40 minutes. Top with Cheddar cheese and continue baking 5 minutes.

Total Microwave Cooking Time 22 to 28 Minutes
Total Combination Cooking Time 28 to 33 Minutes
Total Convection Cooking Time 40 to 45 Minutes
Makes 6 servings

Casseroles

Yellow Squash Casserole

6 cups yellow squash,
   coarsely chopped
½ cup water
1 cup buttery crackers
   (24 crackers), crushed,
   divided
1 (3 oz.) pkg. cream cheese,
   softened
1 (10¾ oz.) can cream of
   chicken soup
1 egg, beaten
¼ cup butter, melted
3 small carrots, grated
½ cup onion, finely
   chopped

In 2-quart casserole, combine squash and water. Cover. Microwave at HIGH (10) 8 minutes; stir after 5 minutes. Drain well and set aside.

Place metal accessory rack on turntable. Preheat oven to 375°F. Place ½ cup cracker crumbs in greased 2-quart oblong glass baking dish. In medium mixing bowl, combine cream cheese, soup, egg and butter. Stir until smooth. Stir in squash, carrots and onion. Spoon into prepared baking dish; sprinkle with remaining cracker crumbs. Convection Bake 40 to 45 minutes.

TO COOK BY COMBINATION: Place metal accessory rack on turntable. Preheat oven to 350°F. Cook on Combination 20 to 25 minutes.

Total Convection Cooking Time 30 to 40 Minutes
Total Combination Cooking Time 20 to 25 Minutes
Makes 6 to 8 servings

Creamed Spaghetti with Turkey Casserole

1¼ cups spaghetti, broken
   into 2-inch pieces,
   cooked and drained
1½ cups cooked turkey,
   cubed
⅓ cup onion, chopped
⅓ cup water
¼ cup green pepper,
   chopped
1 (2 oz.) jar sliced pimento
1 (10¾ oz.) can cream of
   mushroom soup
¼ teaspoon salt
¼ teaspoon pepper
2 cups Cheddar cheese,
   shredded

In 2-quart oblong glass baking dish, combine spaghetti, turkey, onion, water, green pepper, pimento, soup, salt, pepper and cheese. Mix well. Microwave at MEDIUM HIGH (7) 18 to 21 minutes.

TO COOK BY COMBINATION: Place metal accessory rack on turntable. Preheat oven to 350°F. Bake on Combination 30 to 35 minutes.

Total Microwave Cooking Time 18 to 21 Minutes
Total Combination Cooking Time 30 to 35 Minutes
Makes 6 servings

Layered Supper

2 medium potatoes, sliced
2 medium carrots, sliced
⅓ cup long grain rice
2 small onions, sliced
1 lb. ground beef, cooked
   and drained
1 (28 oz.) can tomatoes
2 tablespoons brown sugar

In 2-quart casserole, layer potatoes, carrots, rice, onions, ground beef and tomatoes. Sprinkle brown sugar on top; cover. Microwave at HIGH (10) 25 to 30 minutes.

TO COOK BY COMBINATION: Place metal accessory rack on turntable. Preheat oven to 350°F. Cook on Combination 45 to 50 minutes.

Total Microwave Cooking Time 25 to 30 Minutes
Total Combination Cooking Time 45 to 50 Minutes
Makes 4 servings

▲ *Tamale Pie*

Tamale Pie

1 lb. ground beef
¼ lb. bulk pork sausage
¼ cup onion, chopped
1 (15¼ oz.) can whole
    kernel corn, drained
1 (14½ oz.) can stewed
    tomatoes, drained
1 (6 oz.) can tomato paste
2 teaspoons chili powder
½ teaspoon garlic salt
1 (2¼ oz.) can sliced ripe
    olives, drained
1 (8½ oz.) pkg. corn
    muffin mix
1 egg
⅓ cup milk
½ cup Cheddar cheese,
    shredded

In 8-inch square baking dish, combine ground beef, sausage and onion. Cover with wax paper. Microwave at HIGH (10) 6 to 8 minutes until meat loses pink color; stir every 3 minutes. Drain. Stir in corn, tomatoes, tomato paste, chili powder, garlic salt and olives. In small mixing bowl, combine corn muffin mix, egg and milk just until moistened. Spread evenly over meat mixture.

Place metal accessory rack on turntable. Preheat oven to 350°F. Convection Bake 25 to 30 minutes until center is set. Sprinkle with cheese. Continue baking 6 to 7 minutes until cheese melts.

TO COOK BY COMBINATION: Place metal accessory rack on turntable. Preheat oven to 400°F. Cook on Combination 18 to 20 minutes. Sprinkle with cheese; continue cooking 3 to 4 minutes until cheese melts.

Evenly spread corn muffin mixture over beef mixture and bake.

Total Convection Cooking Time 31 to 37 Minutes
Total Combination Cooking Time 21 to 24 Minutes
Makes 4 to 6 servings

Casseroles

▲ *Simple Tuna Casserole*

Toss bread cubes in melted butter until coated evenly.

Simple Tuna Casserole

3 tablespoons butter
2 tablespoons onion, chopped
3 tablespoons all-purpose flour
½ teaspoon salt
¼ teaspoon pepper
1½ cups milk
2 (6 oz.) cans tuna, drained
2 cups soft bread cubes
2 tablespoons butter, melted
1 (10 oz.) pkg. frozen peas, thawed
1 medium carrot, shredded
1 cup sharp Cheddar cheese, shredded

In 2-quart casserole, place butter and onion. Microwave at HIGH (10) 2 to 3 minutes until onion is transparent. Add flour, salt, pepper and milk. Stir well to blend. Microwave at HIGH (10) 5 to 6 minutes until thickened, stirring every 2 minutes. Add tuna.

In 8-inch square baking dish, toss bread cubes in melted butter. Add peas and carrot. Pour cream sauce over vegetables and top with cheese.

Place metal accessory rack on turntable. Preheat oven to 350°F. Cook on Combination 18 to 23 minutes.

TO COOK BY CONVECTION: Place metal accessory rack on turntable. Preheat oven to 350°F. Convection Bake 25 to 30 minutes.

Total Combination Cooking Time 18 to 23 Minutes
Total Convection Cooking Time 25 to 30 Minutes
Makes 4 servings

Beef & Vegetable Bake

1½ lbs. ground chuck
1 medium onion, chopped
1 (14½ oz.) can tomatoes
1 (15 oz.) can tomato sauce
1 teaspoon garlic salt
¼ teaspoon pepper
1 (15¼ oz.) can whole kernel corn, drained
3 small zucchini, diced

In 3-quart casserole, combine beef and onion. Microwave at HIGH (10) 5 to 7 minutes; stir after 3 minutes. Drain. Add tomatoes, tomato sauce, garlic salt, pepper, corn and zucchini. Stir well. Cover. Microwave at HIGH (10) 15 to 19 minutes; stir after 9 minutes. Let stand, covered, 5 minutes before serving.

Total Microwave Cooking Time 20 to 26 Minutes
Makes 6 to 8 servings

Hearty Bean Casserole

1½ lbs. ground beef
½ cup catsup
½ teaspoon dry mustard
2 tablespoons vinegar
¼ cup dark molasses
⅓ cup onion, minced
1 (17 oz.) can lima beans,
    drained
1 (15½ oz.) can red kidney
    beans, drained
1 (16 oz.) can pork and
    beans
1 (8 oz.) tomato sauce
½ teaspoon salt

In 3-quart casserole, place ground beef. Microwave at HIGH (10) 6 to 7 minutes until beef is thoroughly cooked, stirring every 2 minutes. Drain. Add catsup, dry mustard, vinegar, molasses, onion, lima beans, kidney beans, pork and beans, tomato sauce and salt; cover. Microwave at MEDIUM HIGH (7) 15 to 18 minutes; stir after 8 minutes.

TO COOK BY COMBINATION: Place metal accessory rack on turntable. Preheat oven to 375°F. Cook on Combination 27 to 32 minutes.

TO COOK BY CONVECTION: Place metal accessory rack on turntable. Preheat oven to 350°F. Convection Bake 35 to 40 minutes.

Total Microwave Cooking Time 21 to 25 Minutes
Total Combination Cooking Time 27 to 32 Minutes
Total Convection Cooking Time 35 to 40 Minutes
Makes 8 servings

Spicy Wild Rice Casserole

1 lb. hot bulk sausage
½ cup celery, chopped
½ cup onion, chopped
½ cup mushrooms, sliced
½ cup green pepper,
    chopped
1½ cups water
1 (10¾ oz.) can cream of
    mushroom soup
1 (6 oz.) pkg. long grain
    and wild rice
1 cup Cheddar cheese,
    shredded

In 2-quart casserole, combine sausage, celery, onion, mushrooms and green pepper. Microwave at HIGH (10) 6 to 8 minutes, stirring every 3 minutes. Drain. Add water, soup, rice and cheese; cover. Place metal accessory rack on turntable. Preheat oven to 350°F. Convection Bake 1 hour. Let stand 5 minutes.

TO COOK BY COMBINATION: Place metal accessory rack on turntable. Preheat oven to 350°F. Cook on Combination 33 to 38 minutes. Let stand 5 minutes before serving.

Total Convection Cooking Time 1 Hour
Total Combination Cooking Time 33 to 38 Minutes
Makes 6 to 8 servings

Spinach and Artichoke Casserole

1 (8 oz.) pkg. cream cheese,
    softened
4 tablespoons melted butter
2 tablespoons mayonnaise
6 tablespoons milk
1 (14 oz.) can artichoke
    hearts, drained
2 (10 oz.) pkgs. frozen
    chopped spinach,
    thawed and drained
⅓ cup grated Parmesan
    cheese

Place metal accessory rack on turntable. Preheat oven to 350°F. In medium mixing bowl, combine cream cheese, butter and mayonnaise. Beat at medium speed of an electric mixer until light and fluffy. Gradually beat in milk.

In 2-quart casserole, place artichokes; top with spinach. Spread cream cheese mixture over spinach. Sprinkle with Parmesan cheese. Convection Bake 25 to 30 minutes until lightly browned.

Total Convection Cooking Time 25 to 30 Minutes
Makes 6 servings

Drain spinach thoroughly before adding to the artichokes.

Casseroles

▲ *Chicken Enchiladas*

Chicken Enchiladas

2 (5 oz.) cans cooked chicken, drained
1 (10¾ oz.) can cream of chicken soup
¾ cup Monterey Jack cheese, shredded
¾ cup Colby cheese, shredded
¼ cup sour cream
2 tablespoons chopped green chilies, drained
2 tablespoons onion, chopped
8 (6-inch) flour tortillas
½ cup Colby cheese, shredded

In a mixing bowl, combine chicken, soup, ¾ cup Monterey Jack cheese, ¾ cup Colby cheese, sour cream, green chilies and onion; mix well. Place about ½ cup mixture on each tortilla; roll up and place seam side down in 2-quart oblong glass baking dish. Place metal accessory rack on turntable. Preheat oven to 350°F. Convection Bake 25 to 35 minutes. Sprinkle with remaining cheese and continue baking 5 minutes longer until cheese is melted.

TO COOK BY COMBINATION: Place metal accessory rack on turntable. Preheat oven to 350°F. Cook on Combination 16 to 19 minutes. Sprinkle with remaining cheese and continue cooking 5 minutes longer until cheese is melted.

Total Convection Cooking Time 30 to 40 Minutes
Total Combination Cooking Time 21 to 24 Minutes
Makes 4 servings

Picante Beef Casserole

1 lb. ground beef
1 cup onion, chopped
1 (11 oz.) can Mexicorn, drained
1 (8 oz.) can tomato sauce
⅔ cup picante sauce
1 (4 oz.) can chopped green chilies, drained
½ teaspoon garlic salt
½ teaspoon chili powder
¼ teaspoon oregano
8 (6-inch) corn tortillas
1 cup Cheddar cheese, shredded, divided

In 2-quart casserole, combine ground beef and onion; cover. Microwave at HIGH (10) 5 to 7 minutes until meat is browned, stirring after 3 minutes. Drain well. Add corn, tomato sauce, picante sauce, green chilies, garlic salt, chili powder and oregano; stir to combine.

Place 4 tortillas on bottom of an 11x7x2-inch glass baking dish. Spread half of meat mixture over tortillas. Sprinkle ½ cup cheese over meat mixture. Repeat layers. Microwave at HIGH (10) 11 to 14 minutes until heated through.

TO COOK BY COMBINATION: Place metal accessory rack on turntable. Preheat oven to 375°F. Cook on Combination 20 to 25 minutes.

Total Microwave Cooking Time 16 to 21 Minutes
Total Combination Cooking Time 20 to 25 Minutes
Makes 6 servings

Place 6 tortillas in dish to start first layer.

Sprinkle first layer with cheese and repeat layers.

Cheesy Chicken Casserole

¼ cup butter
½ cup mushrooms, sliced
⅓ cup green pepper, chopped
¼ cup onion, chopped
6 tablespoons all-purpose flour
1 (14½ oz.) can chicken broth
1 cup milk
½ teaspoon salt
⅛ teaspoon pepper
1 (8 oz.) pkg. medium egg noodles, cooked
3 (5 oz.) cans cooked chicken
½ cup stuffed olives, sliced
1 cup Cheddar cheese, shredded

In 3-quart casserole, combine butter, mushrooms, green pepper and onion. Cover with vented plastic wrap. Microwave at HIGH (10) 4 to 6 minutes until tender, stirring every 2 minutes. Add flour, chicken broth, milk, salt and pepper. Stir well. Microwave at HIGH (10) 4 to 6 minutes, stirring with wire whisk every 2 minutes. Add noodles, chicken and olives. Top with Cheddar cheese. Microwave at HIGH (10) 12 to 15 minutes until heated through.

TO COOK BY COMBINATION: Place metal accessory rack on turntable. Preheat oven to 350°F. Cook on Combination 20 to 24 minutes.

TO COOK BY CONVECTION: Place metal accessory rack on turntable. Preheat oven to 350°F. Convection Bake 25 to 30 minutes.

Total Microwave Cooking Time 20 to 27 Minutes
Total Combination Cooking Time 20 to 24 Minutes
Total Convection Cooking Time 25 to 30 Minutes
Makes 6 servings

Eggs & Cheese

Normandy Omelet

**2 tablespoons butter,
   melted, divided**
4 eggs, separated
Salt and pepper
**1 cup fresh strawberries,
   sliced**
1 tablespoon honey
Powdered sugar (optional)

In 9-inch pie plate, place 1 tablespoon melted butter. Turn plate to coat bottom. Set aside. In small mixing bowl, beat egg whites until stiff, but not dry. In 4-cup glass measure, beat egg yolks, salt and pepper until thick and lemon-colored. Gently stir egg yolks into egg whites; carefully pour mixture into pie plate. Cover loosely with plastic wrap. Microwave at MEDIUM (5) 4 to 5 minutes. Let stand 2 minutes. With spatula, loosen edges of omelet from plate.

Combine strawberries, honey and remaining butter. Mix well. Spoon strawberries onto half of omelet. Fold other half over strawberries. Sprinkle with powdered sugar, if desired.

TO COOK BY CONVECTION: Place metal accessory rack on turntable. Preheat oven to 325°F. Convection Bake 17 to 22 minutes. With spatula, loosen edges of omelet from plate. Spoon strawberries onto half of omelet. Fold other half over strawberries. Sprinkle with powdered sugar, if desired.

> Total Microwave Cooking Time 4 to 5 Minutes
> Total Convection Cooking Time 17 to 22 Minutes
> Makes 1 serving

Garlic Cheese and Grits Casserole

3 cups hot tap water
¾ cup quick-cooking grits
1 teaspoon salt
¼ cup butter, sliced
**1½ cups sharp Cheddar
   cheese, shredded**
2 eggs, beaten
Milk
¼ teaspoon garlic powder
Dash hot sauce
**½ cup sharp Cheddar
   cheese, shredded**
Paprika

In 3-quart casserole, place water, grits and salt. Microwave at HIGH (10) 11 to 13 minutes; stir after 5 minutes. Add butter and 1½ cups cheese to grits. Stir until cheese is melted. In 1-cup glass measure, beat eggs; add enough milk to total ¾ cup. Add garlic powder and hot sauce. Quickly stir into grits. Pour into well greased 8-inch square baking dish. Sprinkle ½ cup cheese over top. Sprinkle with paprika. Place metal accessory rack on turntable. Preheat oven to 350°F. Cook on Combination 30 to 35 minutes until knife inserted in center comes out clean. Let stand 5 minutes before serving.

TO COOK BY CONVECTION: Place metal accessory rack on turntable. Preheat oven to 350°F. Convection Bake 35 to 40 minutes until knife inserted in center comes out clean.

> Total Combination Cooking Time 30 to 35 Minutes
> Total Convection Cooking Time 35 to 40 Minutes
> Makes 6 servings

◀ *Normandy Omelet*

Eggs & Cheese

▲ *Make-Ahead French Toast*

Basic Omelet

1 tablespoon butter
3 eggs, room temperature
1 tablespoon water
⅛ teaspoon salt
Dash pepper

In 9-inch pie plate, place butter. Microwave at HIGH (10) ¾ to 1 minute until melted. Turn plate to coat bottom. In medium mixing bowl, combine eggs, water, salt and pepper. Beat with a wire whisk until blended. Pour mixture into pie plate. Cover with plastic wrap. Microwave at MEDIUM HIGH (7) 2½ to 3 minutes until omelet is almost set. Let stand, covered, 2 minutes. Using a spatula, loosen edges of omelet from plate; fold over and serve.

Total Microwave Cooking Time 3¼ to 4 Minutes
Makes 1 serving

Garlic & Potato Omelet

1 small new potato, sliced
1 slice bacon, cooked and diced
1 tablespoon green onion, chopped
⅛ teaspoon garlic salt
Dash pepper

In 1-quart casserole, place potato slices. Microwave at HIGH (10) 2 to 3 minutes until tender. Add bacon, onion, garlic salt and pepper. Microwave at HIGH (10) 1 to 2 minutes until heated through. Prepare Basic Omelet. Fill omelet with potato mixture and fold over to serve.

Total Microwave Cooking Time 3 to 5 Minutes
Makes 1 serving

Make-Ahead French Toast

3 eggs
1 cup milk
2 tablespoons sugar
¼ teaspoon cinnamon
⅛ teaspoon nutmeg
½ teaspoon vanilla
10 slices French bread,
    1-inch thick
Powdered Sugar

Raspberry-Orange Sauce:

1 (10 oz.) pkg. frozen
    raspberries in syrup,
    thawed
Water
⅓ cup seedless red
    raspberry jam
1 tablespoon cornstarch
1 (11 oz.) can Mandarin
    oranges, drained
2 teaspoons grated
    orange rind

Grease a 12-inch pizza pan. In large bowl, combine eggs, milk, sugar, cinnamon, nutmeg and vanilla; beat until well blended. Arrange bread slices on prepared pan. Gradually pour egg mixture evenly over bread, lifting and moving bread slices until all liquid is absorbed. Cover and refrigerate overnight.

Place metal accessory rack on turntable. Preheat oven to 450°F. Remove bread slices from refrigerator; uncover. Convection Bake 10 minutes. Turn over and continue baking 15 to 18 minutes until golden brown. Sprinkle with powdered sugar and serve with Raspberry-Orange Sauce.

Total Convection Cooking Time 25 to 28 Minutes
Makes 4 to 6 servings

Raspberry-Orange Sauce: Drain raspberries; reserve syrup. Set raspberries aside. Add water to syrup to make ¾ cup. In 1-quart casserole, combine syrup mixture, jam and cornstarch; stir until smooth. Microwave at HIGH (10) 3 to 4 minutes until thickened, stirring after 2 minutes. Gently stir in raspberries, oranges and orange rind.

Total Microwave Cooking Time 2 to 4 Minutes
Makes about 2 cups

Pour egg mixture evenly over bread slices.

Lift or rearrange bread slices until all liquid is absorbed.

Cheese Rarebit

8 oz. pasteurized processed
    cheese, diced
1 tablespoon butter
½ teaspoon
    Worcestershire sauce
¼ teaspoon salt
¼ teaspoon dry mustard
Dash cayenne pepper
¼ cup half & half
1 egg yolk, beaten

In 1-quart casserole, place cheese and butter. Microwave at HIGH (10) 2 minutes until smooth, stirring every minute. Add Worcestershire sauce, salt, mustard and cayenne pepper. Quickly stir in half & half and egg yolk. Microwave at MEDIUM (5) 3 to 5 minutes until hot, stirring every minute. Serve over toast.

Total Microwave Cooking Time 5 to 7 Minutes
Makes 3 to 4 servings

Eggs & Cheese

▲ *Ham and Egg Casserole*

Ham and Egg Casserole

**3 cups white bread cubes,
    crusts removed**
**2 cups sharp Cheddar
    cheese, shredded**
**¼ cup green onion, finely
    chopped**
**1 (4½ oz.) can sliced
    mushrooms, drained**
**1 cup ham, cut into
    ½-inch cubes**
4 eggs
½ cup milk
1 teaspoon dry mustard
⅛ teaspoon pepper
Dash hot sauce

In 2-quart oblong glass baking dish, place bread. Sprinkle with cheese, green onion and mushrooms. Top with ham cubes. Beat together eggs, milk, dry mustard, pepper and hot sauce. Pour over ham. Cover with wax paper. Microwave at MEDIUM HIGH (7) 12 to 15 minutes until knife inserted in center comes out clean. Let stand 5 minutes.

TO COOK BY COMBINATION: Place metal accessory rack on turntable. Preheat oven to 350°F. Cook on Combination 21 to 26 minutes, uncovered, until knife inserted in center comes out clean. Let stand 5 minutes.

TO COOK BY CONVECTION: Place metal accessory rack on turntable. Preheat oven to 350°F. Convection Bake 30 to 35 minutes, uncovered, until knife inserted in center comes out clean.

Total Microwave Cooking Time 12 to 15 Minutes
Total Combination Cooking Time 21 to 26 Minutes
Total Convection Cooking Time 30 to 35 Minutes
Makes 4 to 6 servings

Corn and Cheese Souffle

¼ cup butter, melted
¼ cup all-purpose flour
¼ teaspoon salt
⅛ teaspoon white pepper
1½ cups milk
2 cups Cheddar cheese, shredded
1 (8¾ oz.) can whole kernel corn, drained
6 eggs, separated
½ teaspoon cream of tartar

In 2-quart casserole, combine butter, flour, salt and pepper. Gradually stir in milk. Microwave at HIGH (10) 3 to 5 minutes until slightly thickened, stirring every 2 minutes. Add cheese and corn. Microwave at HIGH (10) 2 minutes; stir to blend. In small mixing bowl, beat egg yolks until thick and lemon-colored. Stir in a small amount of cheese sauce; return yolk mixture to sauce, blending well. Cool slightly.

Place metal accessory rack on turntable. Preheat oven to 350°F. In medium mixing bowl, beat egg whites and cream of tartar until stiff peaks form. Gently fold ¼ of egg whites into cheese sauce, then fold cheese mixture into remaining egg whites. Pour into greased 2-quart souffle dish. Convection bake 50 to 55 minutes until top is puffed and golden and center is set. Serve immediately.

Total Convection Cooking Time 50 to 55 Minutes
Makes 6 servings

Beat egg whites until soft peaks form.

Pepper Cheese Pizza

1 tablespoon olive oil
1 medium onion, thinly sliced
½ cup sweet red pepper, cut into thin 2-inch strips
½ cup green pepper, cut into thin 2-inch strips
½ teaspoon hot sauce
1 (8 oz.) pkg refrigerated crescent rolls
½ cup grated Parmesan cheese
1½ cups Monterey Jack cheese, shredded

In 2-quart casserole, combine oil, onion and peppers. Microwave at HIGH (10) 4 to 6 minutes, stirring every 2 minutes. Add hot sauce. Place metal accessory rack on turntable. Preheat oven to 425°F. Grease a 12-inch pizza pan. Press crescent roll dough onto pan. Bake for 5 minutes. Sprinkle with Parmesan cheese. Top with onion, peppers and Monterey Jack cheese. Convection Bake 20 to 25 minutes until cheese begins to brown.

Total Convection Cooking Time 20 to 25 Minutes
Makes 6 servings

Gently stir egg whites into cheese sauce to blend.

Swiss Cheese Fondue

4 cups Swiss cheese, shredded
¼ cup all-purpose flour
⅛ teaspoon garlic powder
⅛ teaspoon pepper
Dash nutmeg
1 cup white wine
French bread, cut into cubes

In medium mixing bowl, toss cheese with flour, garlic powder, pepper and nutmeg. In 2-quart casserole, Microwave wine at HIGH (10) 2 to 3 minutes. Gradually add 2 cups cheese; stir until smooth. Microwave at MEDIUM (5) 2 to 3 minutes; stir after 1 minute. Add remaining cheese; stir until smooth. Microwave at MEDIUM (5) 3 to 4 minutes until cheese is melted; stir after 1 minute. Serve with French bread.

Total Microwave Cooking Time 7 to 10 Minutes
Makes 6 servings

Eggs & Cheese

▲ *Vegetable Frittata*

Vegetable Frittata

2 tablespoons butter
1 small onion, sliced
**½ cup fresh mushrooms,
    sliced**
**4 asparagus spears, cut into
    ½-inch pieces**
½ small zucchini, sliced
8 eggs, beaten
½ cup milk
¼ teaspoon salt
⅛ teaspoon pepper
Dash hot sauce

Place butter and onion in 9-inch quiche dish. Microwave at HIGH (10) 2 to 3 minutes. Add mushrooms, asparagus and zucchini. Microwave at HIGH (10) 4 to 5 minutes; stir after 2 minutes. Combine eggs, milk, salt, pepper and hot sauce. Pour over vegetables.

Place metal accessory rack on turntable. Preheat oven to 350°F. Convection Bake 25 to 28 minutes until set.

Total Convection Cooking Time 25 to 28 Minutes
Makes 4 servings

Breakfast Cheese Pizza

Arrange sliced bread, buttered side down, to form crust.

**½ cup fresh mushrooms,
    finely chopped**
3 green onions, chopped
1 tablespoon butter
5 slices bread, buttered
**1 cup Cheddar cheese,
    shredded**
**1 cup Swiss cheese,
    shredded**
**2 tablespoons all-purpose
    flour**
**6 slices bacon, cooked
    and crumbled**
6 eggs
½ cup milk
¼ teaspoon salt
¼ teaspoon pepper

In 2-quart casserole, combine mushrooms, onions and butter. Microwave at HIGH (10) 2 to 3 minutes until onions are transparent and mushrooms are tender. Set aside. Cut bread slices in half diagonally. Arrange, buttered side down, in 10-inch pie plate, forming a crust. Sprinkle onions and mushrooms over bread.

In medium mixing bowl, combine Cheddar cheese, Swiss cheese, flour and bacon. Spread over onions and mushrooms. In small mixing bowl, beat together eggs, milk, salt and pepper. Pour evenly over cheese. Place metal accessory rack on turntable. Preheat oven to 400°F. Convection Bake 25 to 30 minutes until knife inserted in center comes out clean.

Total Convection Cooking Time 25 to 30 Minutes
Makes 4 servings

Spinach Quiche

½ lb. sweet Italian sausage
2 cups sliced fresh
  mushrooms
1 (12 oz.) pkg. frozen
  spinach souffle, thawed
¾ cup Swiss cheese,
  shredded
2 eggs, beaten
3 tablespoons whipping
  cream
½ teaspoon hot sauce
¼ teaspoon pepper
1 (9-inch) deep-dish pie
  crust, baked

In 2-quart casserole, combine sausage and mushrooms. Microwave at HIGH (10) 5 to 7 minutes until mushrooms are tender, stirring after 3 minutes. Drain well. Add spinach souffle, cheese, eggs, cream, hot sauce and pepper. Pour into crust. Microwave at MEDIUM HIGH (7) 12 to 16 minutes until center is set. Let stand 5 minutes.

TO COOK BY COMBINATION: Place metal accessory rack on turntable. Preheat oven to 350°F. Cook on Combination 20 to 25 minutes. Let stand 5 minutes.

TO COOK BY CONVECTION: Place metal accessory rack on turntable. Preheat oven to 350°F. Convection Bake 30 to 35 minutes until knife inserted in center comes out clean. Let stand 5 minutes.

Test for doneness by inserting knife in center. Knife should come out clean.

Total Microwave Cooking Time 17 to 23 Minutes
Total Combination Cooking Time 20 to 25 Minutes
Total Convection Cooking Time 30 to 35 Minutes
Makes 6 servings

Ham & Grits Quiche

1 tablespoon butter
½ cup fresh mushrooms,
  chopped
¼ cup onion, chopped
1 cup half & half
4 eggs, beaten
½ teaspoon dry mustard
¼ teaspoon pepper
¼ teaspoon nutmeg
1½ cups cooked ham,
  chopped
1 (9-inch) deep dish pie
  crust, baked
½ cup Swiss cheese,
  shredded
½ cup Cheddar cheese,
  shredded
6 bacon slices, cooked
  and crumbled
½ cup quick-cooking grits,
  cooked

In 2-quart casserole, combine butter, mushrooms and onion. Microwave at HIGH (10) 3 to 4 minutes until mushrooms and onion are tender. Set aside. In medium mixing bowl, combine half & half, eggs, dry mustard, pepper and nutmeg. Set aside.

Sprinkle ham over crust. Top with half of cheeses and all of bacon. Pour mushroom mixture over bacon. Add grits. Sprinkle with remaining cheeses. Pour cream mixture over cheese. Microwave at MEDIUM HIGH (7) 14 to 18 minutes until center is set. Let stand 5 minutes.

TO COOK BY COMBINATION: Place metal accessory rack on turntable. Preheat oven to 350°F. Cook on Combination 24 to 29 minutes until center is set. Let stand 5 minutes.

TO COOK BY CONVECTION: Place metal accessory rack on turntable. Preheat oven to 350°F. Convection Bake 40 to 45 minutes until center is set. Let stand 5 minutes.

Total Microwave Cooking Time 17 to 22 Minutes
Total Combination Cooking Time 24 to 29 Minutes
Total Convection Cooking Time 40 to 45 Minutes
Makes 6 servings

Sauces

Raisin Sauce

½ cup orange juice
½ cup water
1 tablespoon cornstarch
1 tablespoon rum
 (optional)
½ cup raisins
⅓ cup currant jelly
Dash allspice

In 1½-quart casserole, stir together orange juice, water and cornstarch until blended. Stir in rum, raisins, currant jelly and allspice. Microwave at HIGH (10) 3 to 5 minutes until sauce is thickened, stirring every 2 minutes.

Total Microwave Cooking Time 3 to 5 Minutes
Makes 1½ cups

Barbecue Sauce

2 tablespoons butter
1 small onion, grated
1 cup catsup
⅓ cup white vinegar
¼ cup Worcestershire sauce
½ cup brown sugar, packed
1 tablespoon chili powder
½ teaspoon pepper
¼ teaspoon seasoned salt
⅛ teaspoon garlic powder

In 2-quart casserole, place butter and onion. Microwave at HIGH (10) 2 to 3 minutes until onion is tender. Add catsup, vinegar, Worcestershire sauce, brown sugar, chili powder, pepper, seasoned salt and garlic powder. Microwave at HIGH (10) 5 minutes. Stir and continue to Microwave at MEDIUM HIGH (7) 8 to 10 minutes until sauce is thickened, stirring every 3 minutes.

Total Microwave Cooking Time 15 to 18 Minutes
Makes 2 cups

Homemade Special Spaghetti Sauce

2 tablespoons olive oil
¾ cup onion, chopped
2 cloves garlic, finely
 chopped
1 (28 oz.) can whole
 tomatoes, chopped
1 (6 oz.) can tomato paste
½ cup water
1 bay leaf
½ teaspoon salt
¼ teaspoon basil
¼ teaspoon oregano

In 3-quart casserole, combine oil, onion and garlic. Microwave at HIGH (10) 1 to 2 minutes. Add tomatoes, tomato paste, water, bay leaf, salt, basil and oregano; cover. Microwave at HIGH (10) 6 to 7 minutes; stir after 3 minutes. Continue to Microwave at LOW (3) 25 minutes, stirring every 10 minutes. Discard bay leaf.

Meat Sauce: Add ½ pound ground beef or sausage, cooked and drained.

Total Microwave Cooking Time 32 to 34 Minutes
Makes 1½ quarts

Hot Bacon Sauce

3 tablespoons sugar
1 tablespoon cornstarch
6 tablespoons white
 vinegar
¼ cup water
6 slices bacon, chopped
 and cooked, reserve
 drippings
1 green onion, chopped

In 1½-quart casserole, combine sugar, cornstarch, vinegar, water and bacon drippings. Microwave at HIGH (10) 3 to 4 minutes until sauce thickens; stir after 2 minutes. Stir in bacon and onion. Serve over vegetables or as a dressing for potato or spinach salad.

Total Microwave Cooking Time 3 to 4 Minutes
Makes 1 cup

◀ Raisin Sauce

Sauces

Basic White Sauce

**2 tablespoons butter,
    melted**
**2 tablespoons all-purpose
    flour**
¼ teaspoon salt
1 cup milk

*To make a cheese sauce, add
shredded cheese to the Basic White
Sauce recipe.*

In 1½-quart casserole, combine melted butter, flour and salt. Gradually add milk; stir until smooth. Microwave at HIGH (10) 3 to 4 minutes until sauce is thickened, stirring every minute with a wire whisk.

Cheese Sauce: Stir in ½ to ¾ cup shredded cheese. Microwave at HIGH (10) 1 minute, if necessary, to completely melt cheese.

Curry Sauce: Stir in 1 to 2 teaspoons curry powder.

Horseradish Sauce: Stir in 1 tablespoon prepared horseradish.

Total Microwave Cooking Time 3 to 4 Minutes
Makes 1 cup

Red Clam Sauce

½ teaspoon olive oil
1 clove garlic, minced
**2 (6½ oz.) cans minced
    clams**
2 (8 oz.) cans tomato sauce
2 tablespoons tomato paste
**2 tablespoons fresh parsley,
    snipped**
**2 tablespoons onion,
    chopped**
**2 tablespoons grated
    Parmesan cheese**
½ teaspoon basil
½ teaspoon oregano
⅛ teaspoon pepper

In 2-quart casserole, combine olive oil and garlic. Microwave at MEDIUM HIGH (7) 1 to 2 minutes. Drain clams, reserving juice from one can. Set clams aside.

In small mixing bowl, combine clam juice, tomato sauce, tomato paste, parsley, onion, Parmesan cheese, basil, oregano and pepper; cover. Microwave at MEDIUM HIGH (7) 9 to 11 minutes. Stir in clams and Microwave at HIGH (10) 2 to 3 minutes. Serve over pasta.

Total Microwave Cooking Time 12 to 16 Minutes
Makes 3 cups

White Clam Sauce

2 tablespoons butter
**1 tablespoon onion,
    finely chopped**
**2 (6½ oz.) cans minced
    clams**
¼ cup dry white wine
⅔ cup whipping cream
**2 tablespoons fresh parsley,
    snipped**
¼ teaspoon oregano
**¼ teaspoon lemon peel,
    grated**
⅛ teaspoon garlic powder
⅛ teaspoon salt
⅛ teaspoon pepper

In 1½-quart casserole, place butter and onion. Microwave at HIGH (10) 2 to 3 minutes. Drain clams, reserving juice from one can. Add clams, clam juice, white wine, whipping cream, parsley, oregano, lemon peel, garlic powder, salt and pepper. Stir to blend. Cover and Microwave at HIGH (10) 4 to 6 minutes, stirring every minute. Serve over pasta.

Total Microwave Cooking Time 6 to 9 Minutes
Makes 2 cups

▲ *Vanilla Sauce*

Vanilla Sauce

⅓ **cup sugar**
1½ **tablespoons cornstarch**
1 **cup milk**
1 **tablespoon butter**
1 **teaspoon vanilla**

In 1-quart casserole, combine sugar and cornstarch. Add milk, stirring constantly with a wire whisk until smooth. Microwave at HIGH (10) 3 to 4 minutes until sauce is thickened, stirring every minute with a wire whisk. Blend in butter and vanilla. Refrigerate for 30 minutes.

Total Microwave Cooking Time 3 to 4 Minutes
Makes 1½ cups

Hot Fudge Sauce

1 **cup (6 oz.) semisweet chocolate pieces**
½ **cup light corn syrup**
¼ **cup half & half or milk**
1 **tablespoon butter**
1 **teaspoon vanilla**

In 1½-quart casserole, combine chocolate and corn syrup. Microwave at MEDIUM HIGH (7) 4 to 6 minutes, stirring every 2 minutes. Gradually add half & half; stir until smooth. Blend in butter and vanilla.

Total Microwave Cooking Time 5 to 6 Minutes
Makes 1½ cups

Brandied Cherry Sauce

1 **(17 oz.) can dark sweet pitted cherries in heavy syrup**
½ **cup sugar**
1½ **tablespoons cornstarch**
1 **cup water**
¼ **cup brandy**

Drain cherries, reserving ¼ cup syrup. In 1-quart casserole, combine sugar and cornstarch. Add cherries, syrup and water; stir until smooth. Microwave at HIGH (10) 3 to 4 minutes until thickened, stirring every minute. Spoon cherries over dessert. Microwave brandy in 1-cup glass measure at HIGH (10) 30 to 45 seconds. Remove one tablespoon brandy into metal spoon. Pour remaining brandy over cherries. Ignite brandy in spoon and pour over cherries.

Total Microwave Cooking Time 3½ to 4¾ Minutes
Makes 1½ cups

To flame, carefully ignite warmed brandy in spoon and pour over fruit.

Vegetables

Acorn Squash with Cranberry Filling

2 medium acorn squash
(about 2 lbs.)
1 (16 oz.) can whole
cranberry sauce
1 tablespoon honey
¼ teaspoon allspice

Prick squash several times with fork to allow steam to escape. Place in oven. Microwave at HIGH (10) 15 to 20 minutes until soft when pricked with fork. Turn squash over after 9 minutes. Let stand 5 minutes. Cut in half and remove seeds. Place cut side up in 10-inch pie plate.

In small bowl, combine cranberry sauce, honey and allspice. Spoon into squash halves. Microwave at HIGH (10) 4 to 5 minutes until heated through.

Total Microwave Cooking Time 19 to 25 Minutes
Makes 4 servings

Stir-Fry Vegetables

2 tablespoons vegetable oil
2 tablespoons soy sauce
¼ teaspoon garlic powder
3 medium onions,
quartered lengthwise
2 cups cabbage,
thinly sliced
1 medium green pepper,
cut in ¼-inch strips
1 cup broccoli flowerets
1 cup cauliflower flowerets
2 stalks celery, sliced
⅔ cup carrots, sliced
¼ cup green onion, sliced

In 3-quart casserole, place oil, soy sauce and garlic powder. Microwave at HIGH (10) 1 to 2 minutes until hot. Add onions, cabbage, broccoli, cauliflower, celery, green pepper, carrots and green onion. Toss to coat. Cover. Microwave at HIGH (10) 8 to 10 minutes; stir after 6 minutes. Serve immediately.

Total Microwave Cooking Time 9 to 12 Minutes
Makes 6 to 8 servings

Zesty Tomatoes & Squash

2 tablespoons butter,
melted
1 teaspoon oregano
½ teaspoon basil
½ teaspoon seasoned salt
⅛ teaspoon garlic powder
⅛ teaspoon pepper
2 medium zucchini,
thinly sliced
1 medium yellow squash,
thinly sliced
2 small tomatoes, each cut
into 4 wedges

In 2-quart casserole, combine butter, oregano, basil, seasoned salt, garlic powder and pepper. Add zucchini and yellow squash. Toss to coat. Cover. Microwave at HIGH (10) 8 to 10 minutes until vegetables are tender; stir after 5 minutes. Add tomatoes. Cover; let stand 2 minutes.

Total Microwave Cooking Time 8 to 10 Minutes
Makes 4 servings

◀ *Acorn Squash with Cranberry Filling*

Vegetables

▲ *Asparagus with Mustard Dressing*

Arrange with tips to the center of dish.

Asparagus with Mustard Dressing

½ **cup mayonnaise**
2 **tablespoons onion,**
    finely chopped
1 **tablespoon white wine**
2 **teaspoons prepared**
    mustard
½ **teaspoon soy sauce**
⅛ **teaspoon ginger**
⅛ **teaspoon white pepper**
1 **lb. fresh asparagus**
¼ **cup water**

In 2-cup glass measure, combine mayonnaise, onion, wine, mustard, soy sauce, ginger and pepper. Mix well and refrigerate.

Arrange asparagus in 2-quart oblong glass baking dish with thicker pieces to outside of dish and tips to center. Add water; cover with plastic wrap, turning back one corner to vent. Microwave at HIGH (10) 3 to 4 minutes until crisp-tender. Drain and chill.

Arrange asparagus spears on serving platter. Top with mustard dressing.

Note: Mustard Dressing can also be used as a topping for broccoli, carrots, cauliflower, Brussels sprouts or green beans.

Total Microwave Cooking Time 3 to 4 Minutes
Makes 3 to 4 servings

Asparagus and Cheese Brunch

8 slices bread
1 (19 oz.) can asparagus, drained and cut into 1-inch pieces
2 cups Cheddar cheese, shredded
4 eggs, beaten
2 cups milk
2 tablespoons onion, minced
½ teaspoon salt
¼ teaspoon dry mustard
¼ teaspoon paprika
⅛ teaspoon pepper

Remove crusts from bread and cut into cubes. In an 11x7x2-inch glass baking dish, arrange half the bread. Cover with asparagus and sprinkle with Cheddar cheese. Top with remaining bread. Combine eggs, milk, onion, salt, mustard, paprika and pepper. Pour over casserole. Let stand 20 minutes. Cover with wax paper. Microwave at MEDIUM HIGH (7) 13 to 18 minutes until knife inserted in center comes out clean. Let stand 5 minutes.

TO COOK BY COMBINATION: Place metal accessory rack on turntable. Preheat oven to 350°F. Cook on Combination 28 to 33 minutes until puffed and lightly browned. Let stand 5 minutes.

TO COOK BY CONVECTION: Place metal accessory rack on turntable. Preheat oven to 350°F. Convection Bake 45 to 50 minutes until puffed and lightly browned. Let stand 5 minutes.

Total Microwave Cooking Time 13 to 18 Minutes
Total Combination Cooking Time 28 to 33 Minutes
Total Convection Cooking Time 45 to 50 Minutes
Makes 6 servings

Corn Pudding

2 tablespoons butter, melted
2 tablespoons all-purpose flour
2 tablespoons sugar
½ teaspoon salt
1 cup milk
3 eggs, beaten
1 (15¼ oz.) can whole kernel corn, drained

In 1½-quart casserole, combine butter, flour, sugar, salt, milk, eggs and corn. Microwave at HIGH (10) 10 to 13 minutes until center is barely set.

TO COOK BY COMBINATION: Place metal accessory rack on turntable. Preheat oven to 350°F. Cook on Combination 17 to 22 minutes until center is barely set.

TO COOK BY CONVECTION: Place metal accessory rack on turntable. Preheat oven to 350°F. Convection Bake 35 to 40 minutes until center is barely set.

Total Microwave Cooking Time 10 to 13 Minutes
Total Combination Cooking Time 17 to 22 Minutes
Total Convection Cooking Time 35 to 40 Minutes
Makes 4 to 6 servings

Sweet & Sour Beets

3 tablespoons butter, melted
2 large fresh beets, peeled and grated
2 teaspoons cornstarch
¼ cup water
1 tablespoon vinegar
3 tablespoons sugar

In 2-quart casserole, combine butter and grated beets. Cover. Microwave at MEDIUM (5) 9 to 11 minutes; stir after 5 minutes. In small mixing bowl, dissolve cornstarch in water. Add cornstarch, vinegar and sugar to beets. Mix well. Cover. Microwave at HIGH (10) 2 to 5 minutes; stir after 1 minute.

Total Microwave Cooking Time 11 to 14 Minutes
Makes 4 to 6 servings

Vegetables

Cooked cabbage leaves should be soft and pliable.

Wrap leaf around meat mixture and secure with toothpick.

Cabbage Rolls

8 whole, fresh cabbage
    leaves
½ cup water
1 lb. ground beef
½ cup instant rice
3 tablespoons onion,
    finely chopped
3 tablespoons green
    pepper, finely chopped
½ teaspoon garlic powder
½ teaspoon salt
⅛ teaspoon pepper
½ cup tomato juice
1 (15 oz.) can tomato sauce
3 tablespoons brown sugar
1 tablespoon lemon juice
1 tablespoon
    Worcestershire sauce
¼ teaspoon allspice

In 3-quart casserole, place cabbage leaves and water. Cover. Microwave at HIGH (10) 6 to 8 minutes until leaves are soft and pliable. In medium mixing bowl, combine ground beef, rice, onion, green pepper, salt, garlic powder and pepper. Divide into 8 portions and place one portion on each cabbage leaf. Roll leaf around meat mixture. Secure with a toothpick. Place rolls, seam-side down, in 3-quart casserole.

In small bowl, blend tomato juice, tomato sauce, brown sugar, lemon juice, Worcestershire sauce and allspice. Pour over cabbage rolls. Cover. Microwave at HIGH (10) 14 to 18 minutes, basting rolls with sauce after 7 minutes. Let stand, covered, 5 minutes.

TO COOK BY COMBINATION: Place metal accessory rack on turntable. Preheat oven to 350°F. Cook on Combination 22 to 26 minutes. Baste rolls with sauce after 10 minutes.

TO COOK BY CONVECTION: Place metal accessory rack on turntable. Preheat oven to 350°F. Convection Bake 30 to 35 minutes. Baste rolls with sauce every 15 minutes.

Total Microwave Cooking Time 21 to 26 Minutes
Total Combination Cooking Time 22 to 26 Minutes
Total Convection Cooking Time 30 to 35 Minutes
Makes 4 servings

Delicious Yams

1 (30 oz.) can yams,
    well drained
⅓ cup orange juice
1 tablespoon cornstarch
½ cup brown sugar, packed
2 tablespoons butter,
    melted
½ cup walnuts, coarsely
    chopped
2 teaspoon grated
    orange rind
⅓ cup shredded coconut,
    toasted

Arrange yams in 1½-quart casserole. In medium bowl, combine orange juice and cornstarch; stir until cornstarch is completely dissolved. Blend in brown sugar and butter. Add walnuts and orange rind; pour over yams. Microwave at HIGH (10) 9 to 11 minutes. Sprinkle with toasted coconut before serving.

TO COOK BY COMBINATION: Place metal accessory rack on turntable. Preheat oven to 350°F. Cook on Combination 20 to 25 minutes. Sprinkle with toasted coconut before serving.

TO COOK BY CONVECTION: Place metal accessory rack on turntable. Preheat oven to 350°F. Convection Bake 30 to 35 minutes. Sprinkle with toasted coconut before serving.

Total Microwave Cooking Time 9 to 11 Minutes
Total Combination Cooking Time 20 to 25 Minutes
Total Convection Cooking Time 30 to 35 Minutes
Makes 6 servings

▲ *Cabbage Rolls*

Scalloped Potatoes

¼ cup butter, melted
¼ cup all-purpose flour
2 cups milk
3 tablespoons dried onion flakes
½ teaspoon salt
¼ teaspoon pepper
6 medium potatoes, peeled and thinly sliced
Paprika

In 4-cup glass measure, combine butter and flour; gradually add milk, stirring until smooth. Add onion flakes, salt and pepper. Microwave at MEDIUM HIGH (7) 6 to 8 minutes until sauce is smooth and slightly thickened, stirring every 3 minutes. In 2-quart casserole, alternately layer potatoes and sauce. Cover. Microwave at MEDIUM HIGH (7) 23 to 28 minutes until potatoes are tender. Let stand, covered, 5 minutes. Sprinkle with paprika.

TO COOK BY COMBINATION: Place metal accessory rack on turntable. Preheat oven to 350°F. Cook on Combination 35 to 40 minutes.

Total Microwave Cooking Time 29 to 36 Minutes
Total Combination Cooking Time 35 to 40 Minutes
Makes 6 servings

German Potato Salad

6 medium potatoes, peeled and thinly sliced
¼ cup water
6 slices bacon, cooked, reserve drippings
½ cup green onion, chopped
2 tablespoons all-purpose flour
1 tablespoon sugar
1 teaspoon celery salt
⅛ teaspoon pepper
½ cup water
⅓ cup vinegar

In 2-quart casserole, place potatoes and ¼ cup water; cover. Microwave at HIGH (10) 10 to 15 minutes; stir after 5 minutes. Let stand, covered, 5 minutes.

In 1½ -quart casserole, combine bacon drippings and onion. Microwave at HIGH (10) 2 to 3 minutes until onion is transparent. Stir in flour, sugar, celery salt, pepper, water and vinegar. Microwave at HIGH (10) 3 to 4 minutes; stir after 2 minutes. Crumble bacon over potatoes. Pour sauce over potatoes and bacon; stir well.

Total Microwave Cooking Time 15 to 22 Minutes
Makes 6 servings

Vegetables

▲ *Stuffed Yellow Squash*

Scoop out pulp and seeds leaving ¼-inch thick shell.

Stuffed Yellow Squash

3 large yellow squash
¼ lb. hot bulk sausage
½ cup green pepper, chopped
¼ cup onion, chopped
1 medium tomato, chopped
½ cup grated Parmesan cheese
½ cup mozzarella cheese, shredded

Cut squash in half lengthwise. Scoop out pulp and seeds; discard, leaving ¼-inch thick shell. Set aside. In 1½-quart casserole, combine sausage, onion and green pepper. Cover. Microwave at MEDIUM HIGH (7) 4 to 5 minutes until sausage is brown; stir every 2 minutes. Drain. Add tomato and Parmesan cheese. Stir until well blended.

Spoon mixture evenly into squash shells; place squash in 2-quart oblong glass baking dish. Cover with wax paper. Microwave at HIGH (10) 12 to 15 minutes until squash is tender. Sprinkle with mozzarella cheese. Microwave at HIGH (10) 1 to 2 minutes until cheese is melted.

Total Microwave Cooking Time 17 to 22 Minutes
Makes 6 servings

Golden Stuffed Artichokes

4 medium artichokes
1 cup water
½ teaspoon salt
1 (6 oz.) pkg. chicken-
    flavor stuffing mix
1½ cups water
¼ cup butter
2 small carrots, grated
1 small onion, diced
1 tablespoon olive oil
1 (3¼ oz.) pkg. salted
    cashews

Remove tough outer leaves from artichokes. Snip tips off leaves with scissors and cut off stems. In 3-quart casserole, place artichokes, water and salt. Cover. Microwave at HIGH (10) 10 to 12 minutes. Remove artichokes and place upside down to cool slightly. In 1½-quart casserole, combine vegetable seasoning packet from stuffing mix, water and butter. Cover. Microwave at HIGH (10) 4 to 5 minutes. Stir stuffing crumbs into mixture. Cover and let stand. In 1-quart casserole, combine carrots, onion and oil. Cover. Microwave at HIGH (10) 3 to 4 minutes until vegetables are tender. Add carrot mixture and cashews to stuffing.

Force the center of each artichoke open to form a well. With a spoon, remove the center leaves and the choke (the fuzzy, purple-tinged area covering the base of the artichoke). Fill artichokes with cashew-carrot stuffing. Rearrange in 3-quart casserole. Microwave at HIGH (10) 4 to 6 minutes until heated through.

Total Microwave Cooking Time 21 to 27 Minutes
Makes 4 stuffed artichokes

After initial cooking, turn arti-chokes upside down to partially cool.

Open the center of each artichoke to form a well. Remove the center leaves and the choke (the area covering the heart of the artichoke).

Three Bean Bake

¼ lb. bacon, cooked,
    crumbled, reserve
    drippings
⅓ cup red onion, chopped
¼ cup brown sugar, packed
1 tablespoon cider vinegar
1 teaspoon dry mustard
1 (16 oz.) can pork & beans
1 (15½ oz.) can kidney
    beans, drained
1 (17 oz.) can lima beans,
    drained

In 2-quart oblong glass baking dish, combine 2 tablespoons reserved bacon drippings and onion. Microwave at HIGH (10) 2 to 3 minutes until onion is transparent. Add brown sugar, vinegar, mustard, pork and beans, kidney beans, lima beans and crumbled bacon. Stir well, Microwave at HIGH (10) 10 to 12 minutes; stir after 6 minutes.

TO COOK BY COMBINATION: Place metal accessory rack on turntable. Preheat oven to 350°F. Cook on Combination 18 to 23 minutes.

TO COOK BY CONVECTION: Place metal accessory rack on turntable. Preheat oven to 350°F. Convection Bake 30 to 35 minutes.

Total Microwave Cooking Time 12 to 15 Minutes
Total Combination Cooking Time 18 to 23 Minutes
Total Convection Cooking Time 30 to 35 Minutes
Makes 6 to 8 servings

To eat, pull off leaves and dip in melted butter or favorite sauce.

Parmesan Cheese Potato Slices

2 large baking potatoes,
    sliced ¼-inch thick
2 tablespoons butter,
    melted
⅓ cup grated Parmesan
    cheese

Place metal accessory rack on turntable. Preheat oven to 400°F. Place sliced potatoes on 12-inch pizza pan; brush with butter. Sprinkle Parmesan cheese over potatoes. Convection Bake 25 to 30 minutes.

Total Convection Cooking Time 25 to 30 Minutes
Makes 6 servings

Vegetables

Southern Stuffed Eggplant

1 medium eggplant
2 tablespoons water
¼ cup onion, chopped
2 tablespoons butter
2 teaspoons parsley,
    snipped
1 (10½ oz.) can cream of
    mushroom soup
⅛ teaspoon pepper
1 teaspoon Worcestershire
    sauce
¾ cup butter cracker
    crumbs, divided
½ cup salted peanuts,
    coarsely chopped
½ cup water
Paprika

Scoop out eggplant leaving the outer shell intact and dice the insides to be used in the stuffing.

Cut eggplant in half lengthwise. Scoop out insides, leaving outer shell intact. Dice the scooped-out eggplant. In 2-quart casserole, combine diced eggplant and water. Cover. Microwave at HIGH (10) 5 to 7 minutes; stir after 3 minutes. Drain.

In 1½-quart casserole, place onion, butter and parsley. Microwave at HIGH (10) 2 to 3 minutes until onion is transparent.

Add onion mixture, soup, pepper, Worcestershire sauce, ½ cup cracker crumbs and peanuts to eggplant pieces. Evenly divide filling between the 2 shells. Place in 2-quart oblong glass baking dish. Add ½ cup water to dish. Cover with plastic wrap, turning back one corner to vent. Microwave at HIGH (10) 6 to 8 minutes until hot.

Sprinkle remaining crumbs and paprika over top. Microwave, uncovered, at HIGH (10) 1 to 2 minutes until bubbly.

Total Microwave Cooking Time 15 to 21 Minutes
Makes 4 servings

Cheesy Broccoli

1 (10 oz.) pkg. frozen
    chopped broccoli
1 cup instant rice
1 (10¾ oz.) can cream of
    chicken soup
½ cup milk
1 (8 oz.) jar processed
    cheese spread
¼ teaspoon pepper
½ cup celery, chopped
¼ cup onion, chopped

Place broccoli in 2-quart casserole. Cover. Microwave at HIGH (10) 6 to 7 minutes. Drain. Set aside.

In same 2-quart casserole, combine rice, soup, milk, cheese and pepper. Microwave at HIGH (10) 2 to 3 minutes until cheese melts; stir well.

To cheese mixture, add celery, onion and broccoli. Stir thoroughly. Cover. Microwave at MEDIUM HIGH (7) 14 minutes; remove cover and continue Microwaving at HIGH (10) 3 to 4 minutes until hot. Let stand 5 minutes.

Total Microwave Cooking Time 25 to 28 Minutes
Makes 6 servings

Twice Baked Potatoes

2 large baking potatoes,
    cooked according to
    chart on pg. 99
2 tablespoons butter
¼ cup milk
½ teaspoon salt
¼ teaspoon garlic powder
⅛ teaspoon pepper
½ cup Cheddar cheese,
    shredded

Cut potatoes in half. Scoop out potatoes leaving ¼-inch thick shell. Set aside. In a medium mixing bowl, combine potato pulp, butter, milk, salt, garlic powder and pepper. Whip potatoes with electric mixer at high speed until smooth.

In an 8-inch square baking dish, place potato shells; fill with potato mixture. Sprinkle Cheddar cheese on top. Microwave at HIGH (10) 2 to 3 minutes until cheese is melted and potatoes are hot.

Total Microwave Cooking Time 2 to 3 Minutes
Makes 2 servings

▲ *Wilted Spinach Salad*

Wilted Spinach Salad

3 strips bacon
¼ cup vinegar
2 teaspoons sugar
¼ teaspoon salt
⅛ teaspoon pepper
⅛ teaspoon tarragon
½ cup sliced celery
1 small red onion,
    thinly sliced
1 pkg. fresh spinach leaves,
    torn (about 8 cups total)
2 medium oranges, peeled
    and sliced*
⅓ cup cashews, coarsely
    broken

In 3-quart casserole, snip bacon into 1-inch pieces. Cover with paper towel. Microwave at HIGH (10) 2 to 3 minutes until crisp. With slotted spoon, remove bacon and place on paper towels to drain.

To bacon drippings add vinegar, sugar, salt, pepper and tarragon. Microwave at HIGH (10) 2 to 3 minutes until mixture boils. Stir in celery and onion.

Gradually add spinach to hot dressing, tossing to coat evenly. Add crumbled bacon, orange segments and cashews. Toss again lightly. Serve immediately.

*Substitute 1 (11 oz.) can drained Mandarin oranges, if desired.

Total Microwave Cooking Time 4 to 6 Minutes
Makes 8 to 10 servings

Vegetables

Vegetable Microwaving Guide

1. Salt vegetables after cooking to avoid dark or dry spots.
2. Arrange vegetables, such as asparagus, with the thickest pieces to the outside of the dish.
3. Cover vegetables with casserole lid when cooking. If using plastic wrap, turn back corner to vent.
4. Large vegetable pieces take longer to cook than smaller pieces.
5. For more even heating, stir vegetables during cooking.

VEGETABLE		Amount	Procedure/Comments	Power Level	Time, Minutes
Artichokes	Fresh	4 medium	In 3-quart casserole, place 1 cup water.	High (10)	14 to 18
Asparagus	Fresh Cuts	1 lb. (3 cups, cut into 1 to 2-inch pieces)	In 2-quart casserole, place ¼ cup water.	High (10)	5 to 7
	Spears	1 lb.	In 1½-quart oblong glass baking dish, place ¼ cup water.	Medium High (7)	6 to 8
	Frozen Spears	10-oz. pkg.	In 1-qt. casserole	High (10)	6 to 8
Beans	Fresh Green	1 lb., cut in half	In 1½-quart casserole, place ½ cup water.	High (10)	12 to 16
	Frozen Green	10-oz. pkg.	In 1-quart casserole, place 2 tablespoons water.	High (10)	6 to 8
	Frozen Lima	10-oz. pkg.	In 1-quart casserole, place ¼ cup water.	High (10)	6 to 8
Beets	Fresh Whole	1 bunch	In 2-quart casserole, place ½ cup water.	High (10)	20 to 25
Broccoli	Fresh Spears	1 bunch (1¼ to 1½ lbs.)	In 2-quart oblong glass baking dish, place ¼ cup water. Cover with vented plastic wrap.	High (10)	9 to 12
	Cut	1 bunch (1¼ to 1½ lbs.)	In 2-quart casserole, place ½ cup water.	High (10)	10 to 12
	Frozen Chopped	10-oz. pkg.	In 1-quart casserole	High (10)	6 to 8
	Spears	10-oz. pkg.	In 1-quart casserole, place 3 tablespoons water.	High (10)	6 to 8
Brussels Sprouts	Fresh	1 lb.	In 1½-quart casserole, place ¼ cup water.	High (10)	8 to 10
	Frozen	10-oz. pkg.	In 1-quart casserole, place 2 tablespoons water.	High (10)	7 to 9
Cabbage	Fresh	1 medium head (about 2 lbs.)	In 1½ or 2-quart casserole, place ¼ cup water.	High (10)	7 to 11
	Wedges		In 2 or 3-quart casserole, place ¼ cup water.	High (10)	12 to 14
Carrots	Fresh Sliced	1 lb.	In 1½-quart casserole, place ¼ cup water.	High (10)	7 to 10
	Frozen	10-oz. pkg.	In 1-quart casserole, place 2 tablespoons water.	High (10)	6 to 8
Cauliflower	Fresh Whole	1 medium head	In 1½-quart casserole, place ½ cup water.	High (10)	10 to 14
	Flowerets	1 medium head		High (10)	10 to 14
	Frozen	10-oz. pkg.	In 1-quart casserole, place 2 tablespoons water.	High (10)	6 to 8

VEGETABLE		Amount	Procedure/Comments	Power Level	Time, Minutes
Corn	**Frozen Kernel**	10-oz. pkg.	In 1-quart casserole, place 2 tablespoons water.	High (10)	6 to 8
Corn on the Cob	**Fresh**	1 to 5 ears	In 2-quart oblong glass baking dish, place corn. If corn is in husk, use no water; if corn has been husked, add ¼ cup water. Cover with vented plastic wrap.	High (10)	3 to 4 per ear
	Frozen	1 ear	In 2-quart oblong glass baking dish.	High (10)	6 to 7
		2 to 6 ears		High (10)	3 to 4 per ear
Eggplant	**Fresh**	1 medium (about 1 lb.)	In 2-quart casserole, place 3 tablespoons water. Add peeled and diced eggplant.	High (10)	6 to 8
Okra	**Frozen**	10-oz. pkg.	In 1-quart casserole, place 2 tablespoons water.	High (10)	6 to 8
Parsnips	**Fresh**	1 lb.	In 1½-quart casserole, place ¼ cup water	High (10)	7 to 10
Peas	**Fresh Shelled**	2-lbs. unshelled	In 1-quart casserole, place ¼ cup water.	High (10)	10 to 13
	Frozen	10-oz. pkg.	In 1-quart casserole, place 2 tablespoons water.	High (10)	6 to 8
Potatoes	**Fresh Whole Sweet or White**	1 (6 to 8-oz. each)	Pierce with cooking fork. Place on paper towel in microwave oven, 1-inch apart in circular arrangement.	High (10)	3 to 5
		4		High (10)	15 to 17
	Fresh Cubed White	4 potatoes (6 to 8-oz. each)	Peel, cut into 1-inch cubes. Place in 2-quart casserole with ½ cup water.	High (10)	10 to 12
Spinach	**Fresh**	10 to 16-oz.	In 2-quart casserole.	High (10)	5 to 7
	Frozen Chopped and Leaf	10-oz. pkg.	In 1-quart casserole, place 3 tablespoons water.	High (10)	6 to 8
Squash	**Fresh Summer and Yellow**	1 lb. sliced	In 1½-quart casserole, place ¼ cup water.	High (10)	7 to 10
	Winter Acorn or Butternut	1 to 2 squash (about 1-lb. each)	Cut in half and remove fibrous membranes. In 8-inch square glass baking dish, place squash cut side down.	High (10)	8 to 11
Succotash	**Frozen**	10-oz. pkg.	In 1-quart casserole, place 2 tablespoons water.	High (10)	8 to 10
Turnips	**Fresh**	1 lb. cubed	In 1½-quart casserole, place 3 tablespoons water.	High (10)	10 to 12
Vegetables, Mixed	**Frozen**	10-oz. pkg.	In 1-quart casserole, place 3 tablespoons water.	High (10)	6 to 8

Pastas, Cereals & Grains

Garden Pasta

3 tablespoons butter
¼ cup onion,
    finely chopped
1 clove garlic, minced
3 tablespoons all-purpose
    flour
½ teaspoon salt
½ teaspoon thyme
2 cups milk
6 slices pasteurized
    American cheese,
    cut into pieces
1 (10 oz.) pkg. frozen
    chopped broccoli,
    thawed & well drained
½ lb. carrots, cut julienne
½ lb. zucchini, sliced
½ lb. sliced fresh
    mushrooms
1 (8 oz.) pkg. fettuccine,
    cooked and drained

In 3-quart casserole, combine butter, onion and garlic. Microwave at HIGH (10) 2 to 3 minutes until onion is transparent. Stir in flour, salt and thyme. Gradually stir in milk. Microwave at HIGH (10) 4 to 6 minutes until thickened, stirring every 2 minutes. Blend in cheese, stirring until melted. Set aside.

In 2-quart casserole, combine broccoli, carrots, zucchini and mushrooms. Microwave at HIGH (10) 6 to 8 minutes until vegetables are tender; stir after 3 minutes. Add vegetables to cheese sauce. Mix well. Serve over fettuccine.

Total Microwave Cooking Time 12 to 17 Minutes
Makes 4 to 6 servings

Deluxe Rice

2 tablespoons butter
1 cup onion, chopped
1½ cups instant rice
½ teaspoon salt
1½ cups water
1 (10 oz.) pkg. frozen
    chopped spinach,
    thawed & drained
1 cup Colby cheese,
    shredded
1 (10¾ oz.) can cream of
    mushroom soup
¼ teaspoon hot sauce

In 2-quart casserole, combine butter and onion. Microwave at HIGH (10) 2 to 3 minutes until onion is transparent. Add rice, salt and water. Cover. Microwave at HIGH (10) 3 to 4 minutes. Let stand, covered, 5 minutes. Add spinach, cheese, soup and hot sauce. Mix well. Microwave at MEDIUM (5) 6 to 8 minutes until heated through; stir after 3 minutes. Let stand, covered, 5 minutes.

TO COOK BY CONVECTION: Place metal accessory rack on turntable. Preheat oven to 350°F. Convection Bake 25 to 35 minutes until bubbly.

Total Microwave Cooking Time 11 to 15 Minutes
Total Convection Cooking Time 25 to 35 Minutes
Makes 6 servings

Noodles Alfredo

1 cup grated Parmesan
    cheese
½ cup butter, sliced
½ cup whipping cream
1 tablespoon fresh parsley,
    snipped
3 cups egg noodles, cooked

In 1-quart casserole, combine Parmesan cheese, butter, whipping cream and parsley. Microwave at HIGH (10) 2 to 3 minutes until butter melts, stirring every minute.

Add noodles. Stir to coat. Microwave at MEDIUM HIGH (7) 2 to 3 minutes until heated through.

Total Microwave Cooking Time 4 to 6 Minutes
Makes 4 to 6 servings

Pastas, Cereals & Grains

▲ *Pasta Salad*

Pasta Salad

2 cups fresh snow peas
⅛ cup water
2 cups broccoli flowerets
⅛ cup water
2 cups cherry tomatoes, halved
2 cups sliced fresh mushrooms
½ cup pitted ripe olives, halved
3 oz. pasta twists, cooked
1 tablespoon grated Parmesan cheese
1 cup hot pepper cheese, cubed

In 2-quart casserole, place snow peas and ⅛ cup water. Cover. Microwave at HIGH (10) 2 minutes. Rinse in cold water immediately. Drain and set aside. Repeat same procedure with broccoli. Drain. Add snow peas, tomatoes, mushrooms, olives, pasta, Paremsan cheese and hot pepper cheese. Toss with pasta salad dressing (see below). Chill several hours before serving.

Total Microwave Cooking Time 4 Minutes
Makes 10 to 12 servings

Pasta Salad Dressing:
½ cup green onions, chopped
½ cup vegetable oil
⅛ cup red wine vinegar
2 tablespoons fresh parsley, snipped
2 cloves garlic, minced
2 teaspoons honey-Dijon mustard
1 teaspoon basil
½ teaspoon salt
½ teaspoon white pepper

In a jar, combine green onions, vegetable oil, vinegar, parsley, garlic, mustard, basil, salt and pepper. Cover tightly. Shake vigorously until well mixed.

Makes 1¼ cups

Snow Peas and Mushrooms with Wild Rice

1 (4 oz.) pkg. wild rice
2¾ cups hot tap water
¼ cup carrots, chopped
¼ cup onion, chopped
¼ cup green pepper,
    chopped
⅔ cup long grain white rice
1 teaspoon marjoram
2 (10½ oz.) cans beef broth
3 tablespoons butter
½ lb. fresh snow peas,
    sliced diagonally
    in thirds
½ lb. sliced fresh
    mushrooms

In 2-quart casserole, place wild rice and water. Cover. Microwave at HIGH (10) 17 minutes; stir after 8 minutes. Drain. Add carrots, onion, green pepper, white rice, marjoram and beef broth. Cover. Microwave at HIGH (10) 29 to 32 minutes until liquid is absorbed, stirring every 10 minutes. In 1½-quart casserole, place butter, snow peas and mushrooms; cover. Microwave at HIGH (10) 4 to 6 minutes until tender. Add to rice; mix well.

Total Microwave Cooking Time 50 to 55 Minutes
Makes 6 servings

Drain cooked wild rice before adding other ingredients.

Fettuccine with Onions and Bacon

½ cup onion, chopped
3 slices bacon, chopped
1 clove garlic minced
1 tablespoon butter
½ cup whipping cream
2 tablespoons grated
    Parmesan cheese
2 tablespoons fresh parsley,
    snipped
½ teaspoon pepper
¼ teaspoon salt
1 (8 oz.) pkg. fettuccine,
    cooked and drained
1 tablespoon grated
    Parmesan cheese

In 1½-quart casserole, place onion, bacon, garlic and butter. Microwave at HIGH (10) 4 to 5 minutes; stir after 3 minutes. Add cream, Parmesan cheese, parsley, pepper, salt and fettuccine. Mix well. Microwave at HIGH (10) 2 to 3 minutes until heated through. Sprinkle with remaining Parmesan cheese.

Total Microwave Cooking Time 6 to 8 Minutes
Makes 4 servings

Pilaf

3 tablespooons butter
⅛ cup onion, chopped
⅛ cup green pepper,
    chopped
⅛ cup carrots, shredded
⅛ cup celery, chopped
1 cup water
1 tablespoon instant beef
    bouillon granules
1 cup instant rice

In 1½-quart casserole, combine butter, onion, green pepper, carrots, celery, water, beef bouillon, pepper and rice. Cover. Microwave at HIGH (10) 8 to 10 minutes; stir after 4 minutes. Let stand, covered, 5 minutes.

Total Microwave Cooking Time 8 to 10 Minutes
Makes 4 to 6 servings

▲ *Cheese Stuffed Manicotti*

Stuff cooked manicotti with cheese filling.

Cheese-Stuffed Manicotti

2 cups mozzarella cheese, shredded, divided
1 (15 oz.) carton ricotta cheese
½ cup grated Romano cheese
1 (7¾ oz.) can spinach, drained
½ teaspoon garlic powder
½ teaspoon salt
¼ teaspoon pepper
10 manicotti, cooked
1 (15 oz.) can tomato sauce
¼ teaspoon basil
¼ teaspoon oregano

In medium mixing bowl, combine 1 cup mozzarella, ricotta, Romano, spinach, garlic powder, salt and pepper. Stuff manicotti with cheese mixture. Arrange in 2-quart oblong glass baking dish. Combine tomato sauce, basil and oregano. Pour over manicotti. Sprinkle with remaining mozzarella. Cover with wax paper. Microwave at HIGH (10) 15 to 18 minutes until hot.

TO COOK BY COMBINATION: Place metal accessory rack on turntable. Preheat oven to 350°F. Cook on Combination 25 to 30 minutes.

TO COOK BY CONVECTION: Place metal accessory rack on turntable. Preheat oven to 350°F. Convection Bake 35 to 40 minutes.

Total Microwave Cooking Time 15 to 18 Minutes
Total Combination Cooking Time 25 to 30 Minutes
Total Convection Cooking Time 35 to 40 Minutes
Makes 5 servings

Hoppin' John

1 lb. bulk pork sausage
½ cup onion, chopped
1 (15 oz.) can black-eyed peas, rinsed and drained
1 cup instant rice
3 cups hot water
½ teaspoon salt
½ teaspoon dried red pepper

In 3-quart casserole, place sausage and onion. Microwave at HIGH (10) 6 to 8 minutes until sausage is thoroughly cooked; stir after 4 minutes. Add black-eyed peas, rice, water, salt and red pepper. Cover. Microwave at HIGH (10) 10 to 15 minutes until rice is cooked and most of the liquid is absorbed; stir after 5 minutes. Let stand 5 minutes.

Total Microwave Cooking Time 16 to 23 Minutes
Makes 6 to 8 servings

Savory Tomato Rice

4 strips bacon, cooked and
crumbled
1 (14½ oz.) can tomatoes,
cut up
½ cup long grain rice
½ cup chili sauce
¼ cup green pepper,
finely chopped
2 tablespoons instant
minced onion
1 teaspoon brown sugar
½ teaspoon
Worcestershire sauce
½ teaspoon salt
⅛ teaspoon pepper
2 cups hot tap water

In 2-quart casserole, place bacon, tomatoes, rice, chili
sauce, green pepper, onion, brown sugar,
Worcestershire sauce, salt, pepper and water. Mix well.
Cover. Micro-wave at HIGH (10) 20 to 23 minutes until
rice is done, stirring every 8 minutes.

Stir and let stand, uncovered, 5 minutes before serving.

Total Microwave Cooking Time 20 to 23 Minutes
Makes 4 to 6 servings

*After microwaving, remove cover
and let stand a few minutes before
serving.*

Cheesy Vegetable Rice

1½ cups long grain rice,
cooked
2 cups mozzarella cheese,
shredded, divided
2 small zucchini, thinly
sliced
1 medium tomato, chopped
1 green onion, chopped
¼ cup celery, chopped
1 teaspoon Italian herb
seasoning
1 (8 oz.) carton sour cream

In 1½-quart casserole, place rice. Layer 1 cup cheese,
zucchini, tomato, green onion, celery and Italian
seasoning over rice. Top with remaining cheese. Cover.
Microwave at MEDIUM HIGH (7) 12 to 15 minutes.
Spread sour cream evenly over top. Cover. Microwave at
MEDIUM HIGH (7) 2 minutes. Let stand 5 minutes.

Total Microwave Cooking Time 14 to 17 Minutes
Makes 4 servings

Granola

2¼ cups regular rolled oats
½ cup coconut
½ cup peanuts, coarsely
chopped
⅓ cup sunflower seeds
⅓ cup toasted wheat germ
¾ cup honey or molasses
¼ cup vegetable oil
¾ cup mixed dried fruit bits
½ cup pitted dates, chopped
½ cup miniature chocolate
chips

In large mixing bowl, combine rolled oats, coconut,
peanuts, sunflower seeds and wheat germ. Set aside.
In small mixing bowl, combine honey and vegetable oil.
Pour over oat mixture, stirring well to coat evenly.
Microwave at HIGH (10) 7 to 10 minutes until mixture
is toasted, stirring every 2 minutes. Add dried fruit bits,
dates and chocolate chips. Set aside. Line 3-quart
oblong glass baking dish with foil. Press the granola
mixture into the foil-lined dish. Cool and break into
pieces. Store in an airtight container.

Total Microwave Cooking Time 7 to 10 Minutes
Makes 7 cups

*After cooling, break into pieces and
store in airtight container.*

Breads

Braided Egg Bread

2¾ cups all-purpose flour,
   divided
1 (¼ oz.) envelope
   dry yeast
¾ cup water
3 tablespoons butter
2 tablespoons sugar
¼ teaspoon salt
1 egg, beaten

In large mixing bowl, combine 1 cup flour and yeast. Heat and stir water, butter, sugar and salt until warm (120° to 130°F.). Add to flour mixture along with egg. Beat with electric mixer on low speed for 30 seconds, scraping bowl constantly. Beat on high speed for 3 minutes. Stir in remaining flour to form soft dough. Cover; let rise about 1 hour or until doubled in size. Roll dough out on lightly floured surface into 12x6-inch rectangle. Cut into 3 long strips 12x2-inches each. On lightly greased 12-inch pizza pan, braid the three strips together to make a loaf. Cover; let rise about 1 hour or until doubled in size. Place metal accessory rack on turntable. Preheat oven to 375°F. Convection Bake 18 to 20 minutes.

Total Convection Cooking Time 18 to 20 Minutes
Makes 1 French-style loaf

Walnut-Apricot Twist

Dough:
1 (¼ oz.) envelope
   dry yeast
¼ cup sugar, divided
½ cup warm water
   (110° to 115°F.)
¼ cup butter
2 eggs
¼ teaspoon salt
2 cups all-purpose flour

Filling:
¾ cup dried apricots
¼ cup raisins
1 teaspoon grated
   orange rind
⅛ cup orange juice
2 tablespoons sugar
⅛ cup walnuts, chopped

Glaze:
1 cup powdered sugar
3 teaspoons milk
1 teaspoon vanilla

Sprinkle yeast and 1 tablespoon granulated sugar over water in large mixing bowl; stir to dissolve. Let stand until foamy. Mix in butter, eggs, salt and remaining sugar. Gradually add enough flour to form stiff dough. Cover and chill at least 2 hours.

In 4-cup glass measure, combine apricots, raisins, orange rind, orange juice and 2 tablespoons sugar. Microwave at MEDIUM (5) 5 minutes until mixture thickens, stirring every minute. Grease a 12-inch pizza pan. Divide dough in half. Roll out one half on lightly floured surface into an 8-inch circle. Transfer to pan. Spread filling over dough to within ½-inch of edge. Sprinkle nuts over filling. Roll remainig dough into 8-inch circle. Place on top of filling; press edges to seal. Using lightly floured 2-inch cookie cutter, cut all the way through center of dough; do not remove. Using lightly floured pastry wheel and starting ¼-inch from edge of inner circle, cut all the way through dough to outside edge. Repeat 11 times, spacing cuts 1½-inches apart at outer edge. Pick up end of 1 dough strip, twist once and replace on baking sheet. Repeat with remaining strips. Let dough rise in warm area 35 to 40 minutes or until almost doubled.

Place metal accessory rack on turntable. Preheat oven to 350°F. Convection Bake 15 to 20 minutes until top is golden brown. Combine powdered sugar, whipping cream and vanilla; stir until smooth. Drizzle over warm coffee cake.

Total Convection Cooking Time 15 to 20 Minutes
Makes 1 (10-inch) coffee cake

Breads

▲ *Toasted Coconut Pretzels*

Sausage Dressing

½ lb. bulk pork sausage
1 medium onion,
    finely chopped
1 cup celery,
    finely chopped
3 cups cornbread crumbs
3 slices white bread,
    toasted and cubed
¼ teaspoon seasoned salt
¼ teaspoon basil
¼ teaspoon pepper
1 cup chicken broth
1 egg, beaten

In 2-quart oblong glass baking dish, combine sausage, onions and celery. Cover with vented plastic wrap. Microwave at HIGH (10) 7 to 8 minutes until sausage is brown and vegetables are tender. Drain and return to casserole. Place metal accessory rack on turntable. Preheat oven to 350°F. Add cornbread, bread cubes, seasoned salt, basil, pepper, chicken broth and egg to sausage mixture. Stir well. Cook on Combination 30 to 35 minutes until heated through.

Total Combination Cooking Time 30 to 35 Minutes
Makes 6 to 8 servings

Apple Spice Bread

1 cup all-purpose flour
¾ cup sugar
¾ teaspoon cinnamon
½ teaspoon baking soda
¼ teaspoon salt
¼ cup butter, melted
½ cup applesauce
1 egg, beaten
2 tablespoons burgundy
    wine or apple juice

Combine flour, sugar, cinnamon, baking soda and salt. In medium mixing bowl, combine butter, applesauce, egg and wine. Stir in flour mixture. Pour batter into a lightly greased 9-inch round glass baking dish. Microwave at HIGH (10) 4 to 6 minutes until toothpick inserted in center comes out clean. Cool 15 minutes.

Total Microwave Cooking Time 4 to 6 Minutes
Makes 8 servings

Toasted Coconut Pretzels

3 cups all-purpose flour
½ cup butter, sliced
1 cup whipping cream
¼ cup water
¼ cup granulated sugar
1 (¼ oz.) envelope
　　dry yeast
½ teaspoon salt
3 egg yolks, beaten

Topping:
1 egg white
1 cup coconut, toasted
½ cup brown sugar, packed

Place flour in large mixing bowl. Cut in butter with a pastry blender until mixture resembles coarse meal. Cover and refrigerate. Heat and stir cream, water, sugar, yeast and salt until warm (120° to 130°F.) and yeast is dissolved. Add to flour mixture along with egg yolks, stirring, just until moistened. Cover and refrigerate at least 12 hours.

Punch dough down. Roll out on lightly floured surface into 16-inch square. Fold dough over into 3 equal pieces. Starting at short side, roll dough into a 10x20-inch rectangle. With pizza cutter, cut 10-inch strips approximately ½-inch wide. Form each strip into a pretzel shape. Brush with egg white. Combine coconut and brown sugar; sprinkle over each pretzel. Place metal accessory rack on turntable. Preheat oven to 400°F. Convection Bake 16 to 18 minutes.

Total Convection Cooking Time 16 to 18 Minutes
Makes 20 pretzels

With pizza cutter, cut 10-inch strips approximately ½-inch wide.

Form each strip into a pretzel shape. Pinch ends to seal.

Orange-Nut Muffins

2 cups all-purpose flour
⅓ cup sugar
1 teaspoon baking powder
½ teaspoon baking soda
¼ teaspoon salt
1 cup natural nutty cereal
¾ cup raisins
1 cup orange juice
2 teaspoons grated
　　orange rind
⅓ cup vegetable oil

In large mixing bowl, combine flour, sugar, baking powder, baking soda, salt, cereal and raisins. Combine orange juice, orange rind and vegetable oil; add to dry ingredients. Blend until moistened. Fill paper-lined, microwave-safe muffin cups ½ full. Microwave at HIGH (10) 2 to 3 minutes. Repeat with remaining batter.

TO COOK BY CONVECTION: Place metal accessory rack on turntable. Preheat oven to 375°F. Convection Bake 15 to 20 minutes.

Total Microwave Cooking Time 2 to 3 Minutes
Total Convection Cooking Time 15 to 20 Minutes
Makes 15 to 18 muffins

Zucchini Bread

1¾ cups all-purpose flour
1 teaspoon cinnamon
1 teaspoon baking soda
½ teaspoon salt
1 cup sugar
1 cup zucchini, grated
2 eggs
½ cup vegetable oil
½ cup vanilla yogurt
1 cup pecans, chopped

Place metal accessory rack on turntable. Preheat oven to 350°F. In small mixing bowl, combine flour, cinnamon, baking soda and salt. In medium mixing bowl, combine sugar, zucchini, eggs, oil and yogurt. Add flour mixture; stir well. Fold in nuts. Pour into greased and floured 9x5x3-inch loaf pan. Convection Bake 55 to 60 minutes until toothpick inserted in center comes out clean. Remove from pan and cool on wire rack.

Total Convection Cooking Time 55 to 60 Minutes
Makes 12 to 15 servings

Breads

Spicy Corn Bread Ring

1 cup French-fried onions,
   finely crushed
1 cup self-rising cornmeal
½ cup all-purpose flour
1 teaspoon chili powder
½ teaspoon salt
2 tablespoons onion,
   finely chopped
2 tablespoons honey
2 eggs, beaten
¾ cup buttermilk
2 tablespoons vegetable oil

Coat sides and bottom of ring pan with crushed onions.

Place crushed onions in 9-inch buttered microwave baking ring, reserving ¼ cup. Turn to coat sides and bottom.

In medium mixing bowl, combine cornmeal, flour, chili powder and salt. Add onion, honey, eggs, buttermilk and oil; stir just until combined. Pour batter into prepared ring. Top with reserved onions. Microwave at MEDIUM (5) 7 to 9 minutes.

Total Microwave Cooking Time 7 to 9 Minutes
Makes 1 (9-inch) ring

Dilly-Onion Bread

1 (¼ oz.) envelope
   dry yeast
¼ cup warm water
   (110° to 115°F.)
1 cup small curd cottage
   cheese, room
   temperature
1 egg, beaten
2 tablespoons sugar
2 tablespoons dill seed
1 tablespoon dried onions
2¼ cups all-purpose flour
1 teaspoon salt
¼ teaspoon baking soda
2 tablespoons butter,
   melted

In large mixing bowl, sprinkle yeast over warm water; stir to dissolve. Mix in cottage cheese, egg, sugar, dill seed and dried onions. Combine flour, salt and baking soda. Add to cottage cheese mixture; stir well. Cover. Let rise in warm place 1 hour until double in size. Stir dough down and pour into well-buttered 8-inch souffle dish. Cover. Let rise about 45 minutes or until almost doubled in size. Place metal accessory rack on turntable. Preheat oven to 350°F. Convection Bake 40 to 45 minutes until browned. Brush with melted butter and cool on wire rack.

Total Convection Cooking Time 40 to 45 Minutes
Makes 6 to 8 servings

Strawberry Bread

1½ cups fresh
   strawberries, sliced
⅓ cup milk
2 eggs, beaten
½ teaspoon vanilla
½ cup vegetable oil
1½ cups all-purpose flour
1 cup sugar
1 teaspoon cinnamon
½ teaspoon baking soda
½ teaspoon baking
   powder
¼ teaspoon salt
½ cup walnuts, chopped

Place metal accessory rack on turntable. Preheat oven to 350°F. In large mixing bowl, combine strawberries, milk, eggs, vanilla and oil. In medium mixing bowl, combine flour, sugar, cinnamon, baking soda, baking powder, and salt. Add dry ingredients and walnuts to strawberry mixture; stir well. Pour batter into greased and floured 9x5x3-inch loaf pan. Convection Bake 50 to 60 minutes until toothpick inserted in center comes out clean.

Total Convection Cooking Time 50 to 60 Minutes
Makes 1 (9x5-inch) loaf

Raisin Bran Muffins

1¼ cups all-purpose flour
1 cup bran cereal
½ cup brown sugar, packed
1 teaspoon baking soda
¼ teaspoon salt
1 cup buttermilk
1 egg
¼ cup vegetable oil
½ cup raisins
¼ cup walnuts, chopped

In large mixing bowl, combine flour, cereal, brown sugar, baking soda and salt. Beat buttermilk, egg and oil together. Add to dry ingredients, stirring just until moistened. Stir in raisins and walnuts. Let batter stand 5 minutes. Spoon into paper-lined, microwave-safe muffin pan, filling each cup about half full. Microwave at HIGH (10) 2 to 3 minutes. Repeat with remaining batter.

TO COOK BY CONVECTION: Place metal accessory rack on turntable. Preheat oven to 375°F. Spoon batter into paper-lined muffin pan, filling half full. Convection Bake 18 to 22 minutes.

Total Microwave Cooking Time 2 to 3 Minutes
Total Convection Cooking Time 18 to 22 Minutes
Makes 18 muffins

Surprise Muffins

1 egg, beaten
1 cup milk
¼ cup vegetable oil
2 cups all-purpose flour
¼ cup sugar
2 teaspoons baking powder
½ teaspoon salt
Fruit jelly

Place metal accessory rack on turntable. Preheat oven to 400°F. Grease bottom of muffin cups. In medium mixing bowl, combine egg, milk, oil, flour, sugar, baking powder and salt. Fill muffin cups ½ full. Drop ½ teaspoon jelly in center of batter; add remaining batter to fill cup ⅔ full. Convection Bake 18 to 22 minutes until golden brown.

Total Convection Cooking Time 18 to 22 Minutes
Makes 12 muffins

Drop teaspoon of jelly in center of batter.

Sour Cream Bread

2 cups all-purpose flour
1 cup sugar
1½ teaspoons baking powder
1 teaspoon baking soda
½ cup butter
1 (8 oz.) carton sour cream
3 eggs, beaten
2 teaspoons vanilla
¾ cup pecans, chopped
⅓ cup all-purpose flour
3 tablespoons sugar
3 tablespoons butter

Place metal accessory rack on turntable. Preheat oven to 350°F. Grease a 9x5x3-inch loaf pan. In large mixing bowl, combine 2 cups flour, 1 cup sugar, baking powder and baking soda. Cut in ½ cup butter until mixture resembles coarse meal. Blend in sour cream, eggs and vanilla. Fold in pecans. Pour batter into prepared pan. In small bowl, combine remaining flour and sugar. Cut in remaining butter until mixture resembles coarse crumbs. Sprinkle over batter. Convection Bake 60 to 70 minutes until toothpick inserted in center comes out clean. Cool in pan 10 minutes.

Total Convection Cooking Time 60 to 70 Minutes
Makes 10 servings

Breads

▲ *Banana Muffins*

Banana Muffins

¾ **cup pecans, coarsely
   chopped**
½ **cup oats, uncooked**
½ **cup corn flakes**
1½ **cups all-purpose flour**
1½ **teaspoons baking
   powder**
1 **teaspoon baking soda**
¼ **teaspoon salt**
2 **large ripe bananas,
   mashed**
½ **cup milk**
½ **cup honey**
2 **tablespoons butter,
   melted**
1 **egg**

Place metal accessory rack on turntable. Preheat oven
to 375°F. In large mixing bowl, combine pecans, oats,
corn flakes, flour, baking powder, baking soda and salt.
In medium mixing bowl, beat together bananas, milk,
honey, butter and egg. Add banana mixture to dry
ingredients; stir until moistened. Spoon batter into
paper-lined muffin pans. Convection Bake 15 to 20
minutes until golden brown.

Note: This recipe is appropriate for the two-shelf convection baking feature. Refer to Use and Care Guide.

Total Convection Cooking Time 15 to 20 Minutes
Makes 12 muffins

Buttery Almond Crown

3 cups all-purpose flour
1¼ cups butter, sliced
2 (¼ oz.) envelopes
    dry yeast
¼ cup sugar, divided
¼ cup warm water
    (110° to 115°F.)
½ cup evaporated milk
2 eggs, beaten
½ teaspoon salt
½ teaspoon butter flavoring

Filling:
½ cup butter
½ cup sugar
½ cup almond paste
½ teaspoon almond extract
¼ cup slivered almonds,
    toasted

Place flour in large mixing bowl. Using a pastry blender, cut in butter until mixture resembles coarse crumbs. In medium mixing bowl, sprinkle yeast and 1 tablespoon sugar over warm water; stir to dissolve. Let stand 5 minutes until foamy. Add milk, eggs, salt, butter flavoring and remaining sugar. Pour over flour mixture and stir until flour is just moistened. Cover and refrigerate at least 5 hours or overnight.

To make filling, in medium mixing bowl, cream ½ cup butter, ½ cup sugar, almond paste and almond extract with an electric mixer; set aside. Butter 12-cup Bundt pan and sprinkle bottom with almonds. Set aside. Roll chilled dough out on waxed paper into 27x9-inch rectangle. Spread filling on dough. Cut dough into thirds. Roll each third in jelly roll fashion and cut crosswise into three pieces. Arrange slices cut side down in bottom of Bundt pan. Let rise in warm place about 1½ hours or until almost doubled in size. Place metal accessory rack on turntable. Preheat oven to 350°F. Convection Bake 35 to 40 minutes until top is golden brown. Cool on wire rack.

Total Convection Cooking Time 35 to 40 Minutes
Makes 12 servings

Arrange dough slices cut side down in bottom of pan. Space enenly.

Oatmeal-Orange Coffee Cake

1½ cups all-purpose flour
1 cup oats, uncooked
⅓ cup brown sugar, packed
1 tablespoon baking
    powder
½ teaspoon baking soda
2 ripe bananas, mashed
½ cup orange juice
⅓ cup butter, melted
1 egg, beaten
2 teaspoons grated
    orange rind
½ teaspoon vanilla
½ cup powdered sugar
1 tablespoon orange juice

Place metal accessory rack on turntable. Preheat oven to 350°F. In large mixing bowl, combine flour, oats, brown sugar, baking powder and baking soda. Combine bananas, orange juice, butter, egg, orange rind and vanilla. Add to flour mixture. Mix until moistened. Grease bottom of 9-inch round springform pan. Pour batter into pan. Convection Bake 20 to 25 minutes until golden brown. Cool 10 minutes on wire rack; remove from pan.

In small mixing bowl, combine powdered sugar and orange juice. Drizzle evenly over cake while still warm.

Total Convection Cooking Time 20 to 25 Minutes
Makes 1 (9-inch) coffee cake

Breads

▲ *Cinnamon Bread*

Old Fashioned Biscuits

2 cups all-purpose flour
¼ cup sugar
1 tablespoon baking
  powder
¼ teaspoon salt
¼ cup butter
1 cup whipping cream

Place metal accessory rack on turntable. Preheat oven to 450°F. In large mixing bowl, combine flour, sugar, baking powder and salt. Using a pastry blender, cut in butter until mixture resembles coarse meal. Add cream. Stir until mixture forms stiff dough. Turn dough onto lightly floured surface. Knead to mix thoroughly. Roll out dough to ½-inch thickness. Using a floured 2½-inch biscuit cutter, cut out biscuits. Place on ungreased 12-inch pizza pan, 1-inch apart. Convection Bake 12 to 14 minutes until biscuits are golden brown.

Total Convection Cooking Time 12 to 14 Minutes
Makes about 1 dozen

Banana Bread

¾ cup sugar
½ cup butter
2 ripe bananas, mashed
2 teaspoons lemon juice
⅓ cup milk
2 eggs, beaten
1½ cups all-purpose flour
1 teaspoon baking soda
½ teaspoon baking powder
½ cup walnuts, chopped

Place metal accessory rack on turntable. Preheat oven to 350°F. Grease a 9x5x3-inch loaf pan. In large mixing bowl, cream sugar and butter with an electric mixer. Mix in mashed bananas and lemon juice; add milk and eggs. Combine flour, baking soda and baking powder; add to banana mixture. Blend well. Stir in nuts. Pour into prepared pan. Convection Bake 50 to 60 minutes.

Total Convection Cooking Time 50 to 60 Minutes
Makes 1 (9-inch) loaf

Cinnamon Bread

2½ tablespoons sugar
1½ teaspoons salt
¼ cup shortening
½ cup milk, scalded
¼ cup cold water
1 (¼ oz.) envelope
   dry yeast
2 tablespoons warm water
   (110° to 115°)
1 egg, beaten
2¾ to 3 cups all-purpose
   flour
¼ cup sugar
2 teaspoons cinnamon
1 tablespoon butter,
   softened

In large mixing bowl, combine 2½ tablespoons sugar, salt, shortening and hot milk; stir until shortening melts. Add ¼ cup water. In 1-cup glass measure, dissolve yeast and warm water; add to milk mixture. Add egg; stir well. Add enough flour to form soft dough. Knead on floured surface 3 minutes until smooth. Place in large well-greased mixing bowl greased-side up. Let rise 1 hour until doubled in size; punch down.

In small mixing bowl, combine ¼ cup sugar and cinnamon. On lightly floured surface, roll dough to 10x8-inch rectangle. Spread with butter and sugar-cinnamon mixture. Starting from long side, roll in jelly roll fashion. Place on greased 12-inch pizza pan and let rise until double in size. Place metal accessory rack on turntable. Preheat oven to 375°F. Convection Bake 25 to 30 minutes until golden brown.

Total Convection Cooking Time 25 to 30 Minutes
Makes 1 French-style loaf

Evenly sprinkle sugar-cinnamon mixture over dough.

Mushroom Stuffing

½ lb. sliced fresh
   mushrooms
½ cup onion, chopped
½ cup celery, chopped
½ cup butter
1 egg, beaten
1 (8 oz.) pkg. seasoned
   stuffing mix
1 cup hot water
2 teaspoons instant
   chicken bouillon
   granules
1 teaspoon ground sage
½ teaspoon pepper

In 2-quart casserole, combine mushrooms, onion, celery and butter. Microwave at HIGH (10) 4 to 5 minutes until vegetables are tender. Add egg, stuffing mix, water, bouillon, ground sage and pepper. Microwave at HIGH (10) 5 to 7 minutes until heated through; stir after 2 minutes.

TO COOK BY CONVECTION: Place metal accessory rack on turntable. Preheat oven to 350°F. Convection Bake 30 to 35 minutes.

Total Microwave Cooking Time 9 to 12 Minutes
Total Convection Cooking Time 30 to 35 Minutes
Makes 6 to 8 servings

Starting from long side, roll in jelly roll fashion.

Buttery Batter Bread

1 cup warm milk
   (110° to 115°)
¾ cup butter, melted
¼ cup sugar
1½ teaspoons salt
1 (¼ oz.) pkg. dry yeast
4 cups all-purpose flour,
   divided
4 eggs, slightly beaten

In large mixing bowl, combine milk, butter, sugar and salt. Add yeast; stir to dissolve.

Add 2 cups flour and eggs. Beat with an electric mixer at medium speed 2 minutes until smooth. Stir in remaining flour. Let rise 1 hour. Stir down and pour into well-greased 10-inch tube pan. Cover; let rise about 45 minutes or until double in size. Place metal accessory rack on turntable. Preheat oven to 350°F. Convection Bake 30 to 35 minutes.

Total Convection Cooking Time 30 to 35 Minutes
Makes 1 loaf

Desserts

Fruit Tart

Pastry Cream:
2 cups milk
½ cup sugar
¼ cup all-purpose flour
2 egg yolks, beaten
1 tablespoon butter
2 teaspoons vanilla

Crust:
1⅓ cups all-purpose flour
2 tablespoons sugar
½ teaspoon salt
7 tablespoons butter
1 egg yolk, beaten
2 to 3 tablespoons ice water

Fruit Topping:
**4 kiwi fruits, peeled and
   sliced**
1 pint raspberries
**1 pint strawberries, halved
   lengthwise**
**1 (11 oz.) can Mandarin
   oranges, drained**
**½ cup apricot preserves,
   warmed**

Place milk in medium mixing bowl; microwave at MEDIUM HIGH (7) 6 to 8 minutes until milk is steaming. Add sugar and flour. Microwave at HIGH (10) 2 to 3 minutes, stirring every 30 seconds. Add egg yolks, butter and vanilla. Microwave at HIGH (10) 2 to 3 minutes, stirring every 30 seconds. Cover with plastic wrap and refrigerate until chilled.

In medium mixing bowl, combine flour, sugar and salt. Cut in butter with pastry blender until mixture resembles coarse crumbs. Add egg yolk and water, tossing lightly with fork until mixture is evenly moistened and holds together. Form dough into a ball, flatten slightly. Wrap with plastic wrap and refrigerate 30 minutes.

Place metal accessory rack on turntable. Preheat oven to 425°F. Roll out dough on lightly floured surface to about ⅛-inch thickness. Line bottom and sides of 9-inch fluted tart pan with dough; prick bottom. Line dough with aluminum foil and fill with pie weights or dried beans. Convection Bake 8 minutes. Remove aluminum foil and weights; continue baking 8 to 10 minutes until golden brown. Cool on wire rack. Spread pastry cream in tart shell. Arrange fruit over cream. Brush lightly with apricot preserves.

Total Microwave Cooking Time 10 to 14 Minutes
Total Convection Cooking Time 16 to 18 Minutes
Makes 8 to 10 servings

Pear and Spice Cake

1 (8 oz.) can pears
**1¼ cups brown sugar,
   packed**
⅓ cup vegetable oil
2 eggs
½ teaspoon vanilla
1½ cups all-purpose flour
¾ teaspoon baking soda
¾ teaspoon cinnamon
¼ teaspoon nutmeg
⅛ teaspoon salt
½ cup pecans, chopped

Place metal accessory rack on turntable. Preheat oven to 375°F. Grease and flour a 11x7x2-inch glass baking dish; set aside.

Drain pears, reserving 3 tablespoons syrup. Chop pears and set aside. In large mixing bowl, combine reserved pear syrup, brown sugar, oil, eggs and vanilla. Beat at medium speed of electric mixer until smooth. Combine flour, baking soda, cinnamon, nutmeg and salt. Add to sugar-egg mixture; blend well. Stir in pears and pecans. Pour batter into prepared dish. Convection Bake 38 to 43 minutes until toothpick inserted in center comes out clean.

Total Convection Cooking Time 38 to 43 Minutes
Makes 8 servings

Desserts

▲ *Chocolate Cheesecake*

Use toothpicks as a guide to slice cake evenly.

Boston Cream Pie

1 (8-inch) round yellow layer cake

Filling:
½ cup sugar
2 tablespoons cornstarch
1⅔ cups milk
1 egg, beaten
¾ teaspoon vanilla
¼ teaspoon butter flavoring
1 cup whipping cream, whipped

Glaze:
2 (1 oz.) squares unsweetened chocolate
2 tablespoons butter
1¼ cups powdered sugar, sifted
1 teaspoon vanilla
3 to 4 tablespoons hot water

Prepare layer cake according to Convection Baking Chart, page 134. Cool completely and cut into 2 thin layers.

In 2-quart casserole, combine sugar, cornstarch and milk. Stir well with a wire whisk. Microwave at HIGH (10) 4 to 6 minutes, until thickened, stirring every 2 minutes. Add egg, vanilla and butter flavoring. Cool completely. Fold whipped cream into thickened mixture. Spread filling between cake layers.

In 4-cup glass measure, combine chocolate and butter. Microwave at HIGH (10) 1 to 2 minutes until chocolate is melted. Add powdered sugar and vanilla. Blend in hot water 1 tablespoon at a time until glaze is desired consistency. Spread over top and sides of cake.

Total Microwave Cooking Time 5 to 8 Minutes
Makes 6 to 8 servings.

Chocolate Cheesecake

1¼ cups chocolate wafer crumbs
¼ cup butter, melted
8 (1 oz.) squares semisweet chocolate
3 (8 oz.) pkgs. cream cheese, softened
1 cup sugar
3 eggs
2 tablespoons Kahlua
1 teaspoon vanilla
1½ cups sour cream
½ cup semisweet chocolate chips

In small mixing bowl, combine chocolate wafer crumbs and butter; stir well. Press crumb mixture onto bottom and 1 inch up sides of 9-inch springform pan. Chill. In 1½-quart casserole, place chocolate squares. Microwave at MEDIUM (5) 2½ to 3 minutes until melted. Place metal accessory rack on turntable. Preheat oven to 350°F. In medium mixing bowl, beat together cream cheese and sugar with an electric mixer until light and fluffy. Beat in eggs, melted chocolate, Kahlua and vanilla until smooth. Fold in sour cream. Pour mixture into crumb crust. Convection Bake 1 hour. Turn oven off and let cheesecake stand in oven 30 minutes. Remove and cool completely on wire rack. Cover and chill at least 8 hours. Garnish with chocolate leaves.

To make chocolate leaves: Microwave chocolate chips at MEDIUM (5) 1 minute until melted. Brush chocolate on leaves. Chill until set. Carefully peel leaf away from chocolate.

Total Convection Cooking Time 1 Hour
Makes one 9-inch cheesecake

Melt chocolate chips and gently brush on leaves.

Chill until set and peel chocolate away from leaf.

Bananas Foster

3 medium bananas, peeled
Lemon juice
½ cup pecans, halved
3 tablespoons butter
½ cup brown sugar, firmly packed
½ teaspoon vanilla
2 tablespoons orange or apple juice
2 tablespoons light rum (optional)
Vanilla ice cream

In 9-inch pie plate, slice bananas in half crosswise and then lengthwise. Brush with lemon juice and sprinkle with pecans. In 2-cup glass measure, combine butter, brown sugar, vanilla and orange or apple juice. Microwave at HIGH (10) 1 minute. Pour sauce over bananas. Microwave at HIGH (10) 2 to 3 minutes until bananas are tender. Add rum, if desired. Serve warm with ice cream.

Total Microwave Cooking Time 3 to 4 Minutes
Makes 4 servings

Pecan Pie

3 tablespoons butter, melted
3 eggs, beaten
1 cup light corn syrup
1 cup sugar
1 teaspoon vanilla
1 cup pecan pieces
1 (9-inch) pie shell

Place metal accessory rack on turntable. Preheat oven to 375°F. In large mixing bowl, combine butter, eggs, corn syrup, sugar and vanilla. Blend well. Stir in pecan pieces. Pour filling into pie shell. Convection Bake 50 to 55 minutes until pie is set in the center. Cool.

Total Convection Cooking Time 50 to 55 Minutes
Makes 1 (9-inch) pie

Desserts

Caramel Bundt Cake

1 (18 oz.) box yellow
   cake mix
⅓ cup creamy peanut
   butter
4 eggs
¾ cup water
⅓ cup vegetable oil
1 teaspoon vanilla
1 cup unsalted peanuts,
   chopped
1 cup (6 oz.) semisweet
   chocolate chips

Sprinkle peanuts and chocolate chips over batter. Repeat for layers.

Caramel Glaze:

2 tablespoons butter,
   melted
¾ cup brown sugar, firmly
   packed
1 teaspoon cornstarch
¼ cup whipping cream
½ teaspoon vanilla

Place metal accessory rack on turntable. Preheat oven to 350°F. In large mixing bowl, combine cake mix, peanut butter, eggs, water, oil and vanilla. Beat on medium speed for 3 minutes with an electric mixer. Grease and flour a 12-cup bundt pan. Pour in one-third of the cake batter, sprinkle one-third cup peanuts with one-third cup chocolate chips over batter. Repeat with remaining batter, peanuts and chocolate chips. Convection Bake 35 to 40 minutes. Cool in pan for 10 minutes. Invert onto serving plate. Top with Caramel Glaze.

Total Convection Cooking Time 35 to 40 Minutes
Makes 8 to 10 servings

In 4-cup glass measure, combine butter, brown sugar and cornstarch. Mix until smooth. Gradually add whipping cream, stirring to blend. Microwave at HIGH (10) 2 to 3 minutes until thickened. Stir in vanilla.

Total Microwave Cooking Time 2 to 3 Minutes
Makes 1¼ cups

Pour Caramel Glaze over warm cake.

Cream Puffs

½ cup water
¼ cup butter
½ cup all-purpose flour
⅛ teaspoon salt
2 eggs
Prepared Pastry Cream,
   page 117

To fill, slice off tops and spoon filling into center.

In 2-quart casserole, combine water and butter. Microwave at HIGH (10) 1 to 2 minutes until mixture boils. Beat in flour and salt until dough forms a ball and leaves the sides of the bowl. Microwave at HIGH (10) 1 minute. Place metal accessory rack on turntable. Preheat oven to 400°F. Add eggs to flour mixture one at a time, beating with an electric mixer until smooth and glossy. Drop batter in 6 mounds onto ungreased 12-inch pizza pan. Convection Bake 25 to 30 minutes. Cut slit in side of each puff to allow steam to escape. Bake 5 minutes longer. Remove from pan and cool on wire rack. To fill puffs, slice off tops. Spoon pastry cream into center; replace tops. Serve immediately.

Total Convection Cooking Time 30 to 35 Minutes
Makes 6 servings

▲ *Apple Pie*

Apple Pie

2 lbs. baking apples,
    peeled and sliced
1 tablespoon lemon juice
¾ cup sugar
2 tablespoons all-purpose
    flour
1 teaspoon cinnamon
¼ teaspoon nutmeg
⅛ teaspoon salt
½ teaspoon almond
    extract
½ cup raisins
Butter
1 (2-crust 9-inch) pastry

Place metal accessory rack on turntable. Preheat oven to 400°F. In large mixing bowl, toss sliced apples with lemon juice. In small mixing bowl, combine sugar, flour, cinnamon, nutmeg and salt; add to apples and toss until well coated. Add almond extract and raisins. Pour apple mixture into pastry-lined pie plate. Dot with butter. Top with remaining pastry and flute the edges. Slit top of pastry to vent. Convection Bake 55 to 60 minutes until crust is lightly browned.

Total Convection Cooking Time 55 to 60 Minutes
Makes 8 servings

Mint Chocolate Chip Pie

1 cup sugar
½ cup butter, melted
½ cup all-purpose flour
2 eggs
1 teaspoon peppermint
    extract
1 cup (6 oz.) semisweet
    chocolate chips
1 cup pecans, chopped
1 (9-inch) pie shell

Place metal accessory rack on turntable. Preheat oven to 350°F. In large mixing bowl, combine sugar, butter, flour, eggs, peppermint extract, chocolate chips and pecans. Pour mixture into pie shell. Convection Bake 45 to 50 minutes until filling is gold brown.

Total Convection Cooking Time 45 to 50 Minutes
Makes 8 servings

Desserts

▲ *Peach Torte*

Peach Torte

3 tablespoons butter
½ cup brown sugar,
    firmly packed
1 egg
1 teaspoon vanilla
¾ cup all-purpose flour
¼ teaspoon baking soda
¼ teaspoon salt
½ cup milk
½ cup graham cracker
    crumbs
⅓ cup pecans, chopped
1 cup fresh peaches,
    peeled and sliced
Lemon juice
1 cup whipping cream

Place metal accessory rack on turntable. Preheat oven to 350°F. Grease bottom of 8-inch round cake pan and line with wax paper. In medium mixing bowl, cream butter and brown sugar with an electric mixer until light and fluffy. Add egg and vanilla. Stir well to blend. Gradually blend in flour, baking soda, salt and milk. Fold in cracker crumbs and pecans. Pour batter into pan. Convection Bake 25 to 30 minutes. Cool on wire rack for 5 minutes. Invert onto wire rack and remove wax paper. Cool 10 minutes. Split cake into 2 layers. Brush fresh peaches with lemon juice.

In small mixing bowl, beat whipping cream with an electric mixer until soft peaks form. Spread one-half of whipped cream on bottom layer and top with peach slices, reserving enough peach slices to garnish the top. Add remaining cake layer. Spread remaining whipped cream over top of cake and garnish with reserved peaches. Chill 2 hours.

Total Convection Cooking Time 25 to 30 Minutes
Makes 6 to 8 servings

Sour Cream Cake

1 cup butter
1½ cups sugar
2 eggs
1 cup sour cream
1 teaspoon vanilla
2 cups all-purpose flour
1 teaspoon baking powder
¼ teaspoon salt

Place metal accessory rack on turntable. Preheat oven to 325°F. In medium mixing bowl, cream butter and sugar with an electric mixer until light and fluffy. Beat in eggs, sour cream and vanilla. Gradually add flour, baking powder and salt. Pour batter into well-greased and floured 9-inch bundt pan. Convection Bake 1 hour to 1 hour 10 minutes until toothpick inserted in center comes out clean. Cool on wire rack after removing from pan.

Total Convection Cooking Time 1 Hour to 1 Hour 10 Minutes
Makes about 12 servings

Banana Walnut Tart

3 cups milk
4 egg yolks, beaten
⅔ cup sugar
¼ cup cornstarch
1 (8 oz.) pkg. cream cheese, cut into chunks
2 teaspoons vanilla
1 cup all-purpose flour
⅓ cup walnuts, finely chopped
½ cup butter
2 tablespoons sugar
2 large bananas, peeled and sliced
¾ cup coconut, toasted

In 2-quart casserole, combine milk, egg yolks, sugar and cornstarch. Microwave at MEDIUM HIGH (7) 8 to 10 minutes, stirring every 2 minutes. Add cream cheese; stir with a wire whisk until melted. Stir in vanilla. Microwave at MEDIUM HIGH (7) 6 to 8 minutes until mixture thickens, stirring every 2 minutes. Cover and refrigerate. Place metal accessory rack on turntable. Preheat oven to 325°F. In medium mixing bowl, combine flour, walnuts, butter and sugar. Blend with an electric mixer on low speed to form a soft dough. Press onto bottom of 9-inch round tart pan. Convection Bake 20 to 25 minutes until golden brown. Cool for 10 minutes. Layer bananas onto the crust and top with custard filling. Sprinkle with coconut. Refrigerate for one hour before serving.

Total Microwave Cooking Time 14 to 18 Minutes
Total Convection Cooking Time 20 to 25 Minutes
Makes 8 servings

Lemon Cooler Cookies

1 cup butter, softened
½ cup granulated sugar
1 tablespoon grated lemon rind
1 egg yolk
½ teaspoon lemon extract
½ teaspoon vanilla
2¼ cups all-purpose flour
Granulated sugar
Powdered sugar

Place metal accessory rack on turntable. Preheat oven to 400°F. In medium mixing bowl, cream butter and granulated sugar with an electric mixer until light and fluffy. Beat in lemon rind, egg yolk, lemon extract and vanilla. Gradually add flour and beat until blended. Roll 1 tablespoon of dough to form balls. Place on ungreased 12-inch pizza pan. Dip bottom of 2½-inch round glass into sugar and flatten balls to ¼-inch thickness. Convec-tion Bake 11 to 13 minutes until edges begin to brown. Cool on wire rack. Sprinkle with powdered sugar.

Total Convection Cooking Time 10 to 13 Minutes
Makes about 2½ dozen cookies

Use bottom of glass dipped in sugar to flatten cookies.

Desserts

▲ *Three Layer Brownies, Peanutty Chocolate Chip Cookies and Lemon Squares*

Lemon Squares

1 cup all-purpose flour
¼ cup sugar
Dash salt
⅓ cup butter
2 eggs, beaten
1 cup sugar
3 tablespoons all-purpose
    flour
½ teaspoon baking
    powder
2 tablespoons lemon juice
1 tablespoon grated
    lemon rind

Place metal accessory rack on turntable. Preheat oven to 350°F. In small mixing bowl, combine 1 cup flour, ¼ cup sugar and salt. Cut in butter until mixture is the size of peas. Grease bottom of an 8-inch square baking dish. Press mixture evenly into baking dish. Convection bake 18 to 21 minutes until set.

In medium mixing bowl, blend eggs, 1 cup sugar, 3 tablespoons flour, baking powder, lemon juice and lemon rind. Pour mixture over crust. Return to oven. Convection Bake 28 to 31 minutes until filling is set.

Total Convection Cooking Time 46 to 52 Minutes
Makes 24 bars

Peanutty Chocolate Chip Cookies

1 cup butter, softened
1 cub brown sugar, packed
½ cup granulated sugar
1⅓ cups (12 oz. jar)
    chunky peanut butter
1 egg
1½ teaspoons vanilla
1½ cups all-purpose flour
½ teaspoon baking soda
Dash salt
2 cups (12 oz.) semisweet
    chocolate chips
1 cup dry roasted peanuts,
    chopped

Place metal accessory rack on turntable. Preheat oven to 375°F. Lightly grease 12-inch pizza pan. In medium mixing bowl, cream butter, brown sugar and granulated sugar with an electric mixer until fluffy. Add peanut butter, egg and vanilla; blend well. Combine flour, baking soda and salt. Add to creamed mixture along with chocolate chips and peanuts; stir to combine. For each cookie, place 1 level tablespoon of dough on prepared pan; flatten to ¼-inch thickness. Space cookies about ½-inch apart. Convection Bake 13 to 15 minutes until golden brown. Let stand 3 minutes before removing to wire rack to cool.

Total Convection Cooking Time 14 to 16 Minutes
Makes about 5 dozen cookies

Three Layer Brownies

¾ cup quick-cooking oats
⅛ cup all-purpose flour
⅛ cup brown sugar, packed
¼ teaspoon baking soda
¼ cup butter, melted
1 (1 oz.) square
    unsweetened chocolate
¼ cup butter
⅛ cup granulated sugar
2 tablespoons water
1 egg, beaten
1 teaspoon vanilla
½ cup all-purpose flour
¼ teaspoon baking powder
½ cup pecans, chopped

Frosting:
1 (1 oz.) square
    unsweetened chocolate
1 tablespoon butter
1 cup powdered sugar,
    sifted
½ teaspoon almond extract
2 tablespoons hot water

In small mixing bowl, combine oats, ⅛ cup flour, brown sugar, baking soda and ¼ cup butter. Press mixture into 8-inch square baking dish. Microwave at MEDIUM (5) 3 to 5 minutes, until surface appears dry; turn dish ¼ turn after 2 minutes. Cool on wire rack 10 minutes. In 2-quart casserole, combine 1 square chocolate and ¼ cup butter. Microwave at MEDIUM (5) 2 to 3 minutes until melted. Add granulated sugar, water, egg, vanilla, flour, baking powder and pecans. Mix well. Spread mixture evenly over oat mixture. Microwave at MEDIUM (5) 5 to 7 minutes. Cool. Frost with Chocolate Frosting.

Chocolate Frosting: In 1-quart casserole, combine chocolate and butter. Microwave at MEDIUM (5) 1 to 2 minutes until melted. Add powdered sugar and almond extract. Add hot water, 1 tablespoon at a time, until frosting is spreadable.

Total Microwave Cooking Time 11 to 17 Minutes
Makes about 2 dozen bars

Basic Brownies

2 eggs
1 cup sugar
½ teaspoon salt
1 teaspoon vanilla
½ cup butter, melted
¾ cup all-purpose flour
½ cup cocoa
1 cups nuts, chopped

In small bowl at medium speed of electric mixer, beat together eggs, sugar, salt and vanilla 1 minute or until light. Add melted butter. Continue beating until thoroughly blended. Mix in flour and cocoa at low speed. Stir in nuts. Spread evenly in greased 8-inch square baking dish. Microwave at HIGH (10) 6 to 7 minutes. When done, top looks dry and will spring back when lightly touched. Cut when cool.

Total Microwave Cooking Time 6 to 7 Minutes
Makes 16 brownies

Peanut Brittle

1 cup sugar
½ cup light corn syrup
1 cup dry-roasted peanuts
1 teaspoon butter
1 teaspoon vanilla
1 teaspoon baking soda

In 1½-quart casserole, combine sugar and syrup. Microwave at HIGH (10) 3 minutes. Add peanuts. Microwave at HIGH (10) 4 to 6 minutes, until mixture is light brown, stirring every 2 minutes. Add butter and vanilla; stir well. Add baking soda and gently stir until light and foamy. Pour mixture onto lightly greased cookie sheet. Cool 1 hour. When cool, break into small pieces.

Total Microwave Cooking Time 7 to 9 Minutes
Makes about 1 pound

Desserts

▲ *Fruit-Filled Pineapple*

Fruit-Filled Pineapple

**1 medium-size fresh
  pineapple**
**1 (11 oz.) can Mandarin
  oranges, drained**
1 cup shredded coconut
**½ cup maraschino cherries,
  drained and cut in half**
½ cup orange marmalade
**½ cup sliced almonds,
  toasted**
2 tablespoons light rum

Cut leafy crown off pineapple; reserve for garnish, if desired. Cut pineapple in half lengthwise. Scoop out fruit, leaving ¼-inch shell. Remove woody core from fruit and discard. Cut remaining fruit into chunks.

Combine pineapple chunks, oranges, coconut, cherries, marmalade, almonds, and rum; toss gently. Place shells on 12-inch microwave-safe plate or platter. Divide fruit mixture evenly between shells. Cover with wax paper. Microwave at HIGH (10) 7 to 9 minutes or until heated through.

Total Microwave Cooking Time 7 to 9 Minutes
Makes 6 servings

Turtle Brownies

**25 caramel candies,
  unwrapped**
¼ cup evaporated milk
¼ cup butter, melted
**1 (10¼ oz.) pkg. brownie
  mix**
**2 tablespoons evaporated
  milk**
**½ cup semisweet
  chocolate chips**
½ cup pecans, chopped

In medium mixing bowl, combine caramels and ¼ cup evaporated milk. Microwave at HIGH (10) 2 to 3 minutes, stirring every 30 seconds. In large mixing bowl, combine butter, brownie mix and 2 tablespoons evaporated milk. Press one-half of mixture into lightly greased 8-inch square baking dish. Microwave at HIGH (10) 2 to 3 minutes. Sprinkle chocolate chips and pecans on top. Spread caramel mixture over chocolate chips and pecans. Crumble remaining brownie mix over caramel mixture. Microwave at HIGH (10) 4 to 5 minutes. Cool completely before cutting.

Total Microwave Cooking Time 8 to 11 Minutes
Makes 16 brownies

*To prepare caramel mixture,
combine caramels and evaporated
milk, then microwave.*

Toffee Cake

1½ cups all-purpose flour
1 cup brown sugar, packed
Dash salt
⅛ cup butter
⅔ cup buttermilk
1 egg, beaten
½ teaspoon vanilla
¾ teaspoon baking soda
**3 (1.4 oz.) chocolate
  covered English toffee
  bars, coarsely chopped**
¼ cup walnuts, chopped

Place metal accessory rack on turntable. Preheat oven to 375°F. Grease a 11x7x2-inch cake dish. In large mixing bowl, combine flour, sugar and salt. With a pastry blender, cut in butter until mixture resembles coarse crumbs. Remove ¾ cup flour mixture and place in medium mixing bowl; set aside. Add buttermilk, egg, vanilla and baking soda. Mix until well blended. Pour batter evenly into prepared dish. In medium mixing bowl, mix reserved flour mixture, toffee and walnuts. Sprinkle toffee mixture over batter. Bake 35 to 45 minutes until toothpick inserted in center comes out clean.

Total Convection Cooking Time 35 to 45 Minutes
Makes 8 servings

Chocolate Chip Squares

¾ cup brown sugar, packed
½ cup butter, melted
2 eggs, beaten
1 teaspoon vanilla
**½ cup semisweet chocolate
  chips**
½ cup walnuts, chopped
½ cup all-purpose flour
1 teaspoon baking powder
¼ teaspoon salt

In medium mixing bowl, combine sugar, butter, eggs and vanilla. Stir until blended. Add chocolate chips, walnuts, flour, baking powder and salt. Mix well. Pour batter into 8-inch square glass baking dish. Microwave at HIGH (10) 6 to 8 minutes until toothpick inserted in center comes out clean. Cool completely before cutting.

Total Microwave Cooking Time 6 to 8 Minutes
Makes 16 squares

Microwaving Guide

1. Cook times and food quantities below should be used as a guide. In microwaving, the greater the quantity of food the longer the cook time.
2. Always cook in microwave-safe plastic, glass or oven-safe plastic containers. DO NOT USE METAL CONTAINERS. Refer to Cookware and Utensil Guide on page 5 for detailed information.
3. When covering utensils with plastic wrap, turn one corner back to vent.

4. Since microwaving does not brown or crisp food, you may prefer to convection bake or combination cook foods such as meats and baked goods.
5. Before using microwave plastic containers be sure oven is cool. If still hot from convection or combination cooking, choose glass or oven-safe plastic containers.

FOOD		Cover	Power Level and Time	Comments
Appetizers	Party mix (2½-quarts)	No	High (10) 6 to 7 minutes.	Stir every 2 minutes.
	Meatballs, small meat or hot dog chunks (24)	Wax paper or plastic wrap	High (10) 5 to 6 minutes.	Spread in single layer in 2-quart oblong glass baking dish.
	Stuffed vegetables (12)	No	High (10) 3 to 4 minutes.	Space evenly on trivet or on plate lined with paper towels.
	Toasted nuts or seeds (½ to 1 cup)	No	High (10) 4 to 7 minutes.	Combine nuts with small amount of butter, stirring every 2 minutes.
Cakes, Cookies, Breads	Oblong, square or round	No	Medium High (7) 5 to 7 minutes.	
	Fluted tube cake	No	High (10) 12 to 14 minutes.	Let stand 10 minutes before inverting to cool.
	Cheesecake (9-inch pie plate)	No	Medium High (7) 12 to 14 minutes.	Microwave cheesecake mixture in 2-quart casserole until thick and smooth. Stir every 2 minutes with wire whisk. Pour into crumb crust. Refrigerate until firm.
	Bar Cookies (8-in. square dish)	No	High (10) 6 to 9 minutes.	
	Muffins (6)	No	Medium High (7) 2 to 3 minutes.	Check at minimum time.
Eggs, Cheese, Dairy	Scrambled eggs	No	High (10) Allow ¾ to 1 minute per egg.	Stir 2 or 3 times during microwaving.
	Quiche	No	Medium High (7) 16 to 22 minutes.	Pour filling into prebaked shell.
	Thickened sauces and gravies (1 cup)	No	Medium (5) 3 to 5 minutes.	Microwave fat, flour and salt 1 to 2 minutes; stir to blend. Add liquid. Stir every minute.
	Scald milk (½ cup)	No	Medium High (7) 3 to 5 minutes until steaming.	
	Melt butter (½ cup)	No	High (10) 1 to 2 minutes.	
	Soften cream cheese (8 oz.)	No	Low (3) ½ to 1 minute.	Remove foil wrapper before softening and place on microwave-safe plate.
Fish & Shellfish	Fillets or steaks (1 lb.)	Wax paper	High (10) 5 to 7 minutes.	Very delicate fish should be placed on trivet.
	Casserole, pre-cooked (2 to 3 quart)	Plastic wrap	High (10) 12 to 18 minutes.	
	Scallops, shrimp, peeled (1 lb.)	Plastic wrap	High (10) 5 to 7 minutes.	Brush with garlic butter before cooking.
Fruits	Baked apples or pears	Lid or plastic wrap	High (10) 2 to 3 minutes per piece.	Pierce fruit or peel to prevent bursting.

FOOD		Cover	Power Level and Time	Comments
Meat	Ground meat (1 lb.)	Lid or wax paper	High (10) 5 to 7 minutes.	Break up and stir after 3 minutes.
	Bacon (2 to 8 strips)	Paper towels	High (10) 1 to 1½ minutes per slice.	Place on trivet or on paper towel-lined plate.
	Sausage	Wax paper	High (10) Patties: 1 minute per patty. Links: ½ to ¾ minute per link.	Place on paper towel-lined plate or glass dish. Turn over after half of cooking time.
	Franks or hot dogs (1 lb.)	Lid	High (10) 5 to 7 minutes.	Add ¾ cup water. Rearrange after half of cooking time.
	Sandwiches	Wrap in paper towel	High (10) 1 to 2 minutes per sandwich.	
	Meat casseroles with pre-cooked meat and ingredients	Lid or plastic wrap	High (10) 13 to 19 minutes.	Stir once or twice.
	Meat casseroles with raw meat and vegetables	Lid or wax paper	Ground meat: High (10) 28 to 32 minutes. Less tender chunks: Medium (5) 70 to 75 minutes.	Rearrange or stir after half time.
	Meat patties (4 per 1 lb.)	Wax paper	High (10) 3 to 5 minutes.	Place on trivet or on paper towel-lined plate.
	Meat loaf, beef or ham (1½ lbs. meat)	Plastic wrap	9x5x3-inch loaf dish: Medium High (7) 25 to 30 minutes.	
	Braised (water cooked): short ribs, brisket, spare ribs (2 to 3 lbs.)	Lid or plastic wrap	Medium (5) 80 to 90 minutes.	Cover meat with water. Rearrange after half of cooking time. For ribs, drain 10 minutes before finishing and add barbecue sauce, if desired.
	Chops with sauce (4 1-inch chops)	Wax paper	Medium High (7) 20 to 25 minutes.	Turn over after half of cooking time.
Pasta	Long pieces (spaghetti, etc, ½ lb.)	Plastic wrap	High (10) 12 to 15 minutes.	In 2-quart oblong glass dish, add 6 cups hot tap water, 1 tablespoon oil, 1 teaspoon salt. Rearrange after half of cooking time.
	Cereal or instant rice	Lid or plastic wrap	High (10) 2 to 3 minutes per serving.	Add hot tap water as given on package. Stir after half of cooking time.
Pies	Crumb crust (9-inch)	No	High (10) 1 to 2 minutes.	
Poultry	Chicken, 6 to 8 pieces	Plastic wrap	High (10) 12 to 15 minutes.	Turn over after half of cooking time.
	Chicken, whole or Cornish hens	Cooking Bag	Medium High (7) 8 to 10 minutes per lb.	Place on trivet. Turn over after half of cooking time. Shield tips of wings and legs with foil.
	Turkey breast	Cooking Bag	Medium (5) 11 to 13 minutes per lb.	Place on trivet, breast side down. Turn over after half of cooking time.
Roasts	Pot roast (2½ to 3 lbs.)	Cooking Bag	Low (3) 25 to 28 minutes per lb.	Turn over after half of cooking time.
	Tender beef roast Boneless	Cooking Bag	Medium (5) Rare: 8 to 11 minutes per lb. Medium: 11 to 14 minutes per lb. Well done: 14 to 17 minutes per lb.	Turn over after half of cooking time.
	Bone-in	Cooking Bag	Medium (5) Rare: 7 to 10 minutes per lb. Medium: 10 to 13 minutes per lb. Well done: 13 to 16 minutes per lb.	Turn over after half of cooking time.
	Boneless pork roast	Cooking Bag	Medium (5) 13 to 16 minutes per lb.	Turn over after half of cooking time.
	Bone-in pork roast	Cooking Bag	Medium (5) 12 to 15 minutes per lb.	Turn over after half of cooking time.
	Ham roast, pre-cooked	Plastic wrap	Medium (5) 11 to 14 minutes per lb.	Turn over after half of cooking time.

Defrosting Chart Power Level: Defrost (3)

1. Most foods should be turned over after half of defrosting time.
2. Large foods such as roasts or turkey breast, should stand on countertop for 15 to 30 minutes to complete defrosting.

3. When defrosting steaks or chops, separate and remove defrosted pieces after half of defrost time. Return frozen pieces to oven to complete defrosting.

FOOD		First Half Time, Min.	Second Half Time, Min.	Comments
Breads, Cakes	Bread or buns (1-lb. pkg.)	1 to 2	1 to 2	Turn over after first half of time.
	Heat & serve rolls (7-oz. pkg.)	2 to 3	none	
	Coffee cake (11 to 13 oz.)	4 to 6	none	
	Coffee ring (10-oz. pkg.)	3 to 4	none	
	Sweet rolls (12-oz. pkg.)	3 to 4	none	
	Doughnuts (1 to 3)	¾ to 1	none	
	Doughnuts, glazed (box of 12)	3 to 4		Turn box over after first half of time.
	French toast (2 slices)	1 to 2		
	Cake, frosted 2 to 3 layer (17 to 22 oz.)	2 to 3	none	Let stand 10 minutes before serving.
	Cake, filled or topped 1 layer (12½ to 16 oz.)	2 to 3	none	Let stand 10 minutes before serving.
	Pound cake (11¼ oz.)	2 to 3	none	Let stand 10 minutes before serving.
	Cheesecake, plain or fruit top (17 to 19 oz.)	2 to 3	none	Microwave 1 to 2 minutes more, if needed.
	Crunch cakes & cupcakes (1 to 2)	½ to 1	none	
	Fruit or nut pie (8 inch)	8 to 10	none	
	Cream or custard pie (14 to 24 oz.)	2 to 4	none	Let stand 5 minutes before serving.
Fish & Seafood	Fillets (1 lb.)	4 to 5	5 to 6	Place unopened package in oven. (If fish is frozen in water, place in cooking dish.) Turn over after first half of time. Let stand 5 minutes on counter to complete defrosting.
	Steaks, 4 (5 to 6 oz. each)	5	5	Place wrapped steaks in oven. Turn over and separate after first half of time.
	Whole fish (8 to 10 oz.)	2	3 to 4	Place fish in cooking dish. Turn over after first half of time. After second half of time, rinse cavity with cold water to complete defrosting.
	Shellfish, small pieces (1 lb.)	3 to 4	2 to 3	Spread shellfish in single layer in baking dish. Rearrange pieces after first half of time.
	Shellfish, blocks Crab meat (6-oz. pkg.)	2	2 to 3	Place block in casserole. Turn over and break up with fork after first half of time.
	Oysters (12-oz. can)	5 to 7	5 to 7	Place block in casserole. Turn over and break up with fork after first half of time. Let stand 10 minutes after defrosting.
	Scallops (1-lb. pkg.)	3 to 5	3 to 5	Place block in casserole. Turn over and break up with fork after first half of time. Let stand 10 minutes after defrosting.
	Shellfish, large Crab legs – 1 to 2 (8 to 10 oz.)	2 to 3	2 to 3	Arrange in cooking dish with light underside up. Turn over after first half of time.
	Lobster tails – 1 to 2 (6 to 9 oz.)	3 to 4	3 to 4	Arrange in cooking dish with light underside up. Turn over after first half of time.
	Whole lobster or crab (1½ lbs.)	7 to 8	6 to 8	Place in cooking dish with light underside up. Turn over after first half of time.

FOOD		First Half Time, Min.	Second Half Time, Min.	Comments
Fruit	Fresh (10 to 16 oz.) (In microwave-safe container)	2½	2½	Place package in oven. After first half of time, break up with fork. Let stand on counter to complete defrosting.
	Plastic pouch – 1 to 2 (10-oz. pkg.)	2½	2½ to 5½	Place package in oven. After first half of time, flex package.
Meat	Bacon (1 lb.)	2 to 3 per lb.	1 to 2 per lb.	Place unopened package in oven. Turn over after first half of time. Microwave just until strips can be separated.
	Franks (1 lb.) (½ lb.)	2 to 3 1½ to 2½	2 to 3 none	Place unopened package in oven. Turn over after first half of time. Microwave just until franks can be separated.
	Ground beef or pork (1 lb.)	4	2 to 3	Scrape off meat that softens during defrosting. Set aside. Break up remaining block and continue defrosting.
	(1½ to 2 lbs.)	7	7	Scrape off meat that softens during defrosting. Set aside. Break up remaining block and continue defrosting.
	(5 lbs.)	13	13	Scrape off meat that softens during defrosting. Set aside. Break up remaining block and continue defrosting.
	Roast: beef, lamb or veal	7 per lb.	7 per lb.	Place unwrapped roast in glass casserole; shield ends with foil. Turn over after first (3 to 5 lbs.) half of time and shield warm areas with foil. Let stand 30 minutes.
	Roast, pork (3 to 5 lbs.)	4 to 5 per lb.	3 to 4 per lb.	Place unwrapped roast in glass casserole; shield ends with foil. Turn over after first (3 to 5 lbs.) half of time and shield warm areas with foil. Let stand 30 minutes.
	Spareribs, pork (1½ lbs.)	2 to 4 per lb.	2 to 4 per lb.	Place wrapped package in oven. Turn over after first half of time. After second half of time, unwrap and separate pieces. Let stand to complete defrosting.
	Steaks, chops or cutlets: beef, lamb, pork & veal	3 to 5 per lb.	3 to 5 per lb.	Place wrapped package in oven. Turn over after first half of time. After second half of time, unwrap and separate pieces. Let stand to complete defrosting.
	Sausage, bulk (1-lb. roll)	2 to 3	2 to 3	Scrape off softened meat after first half of time. Set aside. Break up remaining block and continue defrosting.
	Sausage, link (½ to 1 lb.)	2	1 to 2	Turn over after first half of time.
	Sausage, patties (12-oz. pkg.)	2	1 to 2	Turn over and separate after first half of time.
Poultry	Chicken, cut up (2½ to 3½ lbs.)	6 to 8	6 to 8	Place wrapped chicken in oven. After first half of time, unwrap, turn over and separate pieces.
	Chicken, whole (2½ to 3½ lbs.)	10 to 12	10 to 12	Place wrapped chicken in oven. After first half of time, unwrap and turn over. Shield warm areas with foil. Let stand 15 minutes.
	Cornish hen	3 to 4 per lb.	3 to 4 per lb.	Place wrapped package in oven. Turn over after first half of time. After second half of time, unwrap and shield warm areas and ends of legs with foil. Microwave 3 to 4 minutes more, if necessary.
	Duckling	4 to 6 per lb.	4 to 6 per lb.	Place wrapped duckling in oven. After first half of time, unwrap, turn over and place in cooking dish. Shield warm areas and ends of legs with foil.
	Turkey breast	3 to 5 per lb.	3 to 4 per lb.	Place unwrapped turkey, breast side down, in cooking dish. After first half of time, turn turkey breast side up and shield with foil. Let stand 30 minutes.

Heating or Reheating Chart

1. Directions below are for reheating cooked foods at refrigerator or room temperature. Use microwave oven-safe containers.
2. Cover most foods for fastest heating. Exceptions are rare or medium rare meats, some sandwiches, griddle foods such as pancakes and baked foods.
3. Edges of food will heat faster than center. Stir foods before serving whenever possible.

4. Stir or rearrange large amounts of food after half the suggested heating time.
5. Be sure foods are heated through before serving. Steaming or bubbling around edges does not necessarily mean food is heated in center. As a general rule, hot foods produce an area warm to the touch in center of underside of dish.
6. When covering with plastic wrap, turn back one corner to vent.

Item		Amount	Power Level	Approx. Time, Minutes
Appetizers	Saucy such as: meatballs, riblets, cocktail franks, etc. ½ cup / serving	1 to 2 servings 3 to 4 servings	High (10) High (10)	2 to 3 3 to 4
	Dips: cream or process cheese	½ cup 1 cup	Medium (5) Medium (5)	1 to 2 2 to 3
	Pastry bites: small pizzas, egg rolls etc.	2 to 4 servings	High (10)	1 to 3
	Tip: Cover saucy appetizers with wax paper. Cover dips with plastic wrap. Do not cover pastry bites.			
Plate of Leftovers	Meat plus 2 vegetables	1 plate	High (10)	1 to 3
	Tip: Cover plate of food with wax paper or plastic wrap.			
Meats & Main Dishes	Saucy Main Dishes: chop suey, spaghetti, creamed chicken, chili, stew, macaroni and cheese, etc. ¾ - 1 cup / serving	1 to 2 servings 3 to 4 servings 1 16-oz. can	High (10) High (10) High (10)	2 to 3 3 to 4 4 to 5
	Thinly sliced roasted meat: Rare, minimum time Medium Rare, maximum time 3 to 4-oz. / serving	1 to 2 servings 3 to 4 servings	Medium High (7) Medium High (7)	1 to 2 2 to 3
	Well done beef, pork, ham, poultry, etc. 3 to 4-oz. / serving	1 to 2 servings 3 to 4 servings	Medium High (7) Medium High (7)	1 to 3 3 to 4
	Steaks, chops, ribs, other meat pieces:			
	Rare beef steak	1 to 2 servings 3 to 4 servings	Medium High (7) Medium High (7)	1 to 2 2 to 3
	Well done beef, chops, ribs, etc.	1 to 2 servings 4 servings	Medium High (7) Medium High (7)	1 to 2 2 to 4
	Hamburgers or meat loaf 4-oz. / serving	1 to 2 servings 3 to 4 servings	High (10) High (10)	1 to 2 2 to 3
	Chicken pieces	1 to 2 pieces 3 to 4 pieces	High (10) High (10)	1 to 2 2 to 3
	Hot dogs and sausages	1 to 2 3 to 4	High (10) High (10)	½ to 1½ 1½ to 2
	Rice and pasta Plain or buttered ½ to 1 cup / serving	1 to 2 servings 3 to 4 servings	High (10) High (10)	1 to 2 2 to 3
	Topped or mixed with sauce ½ to 1 cup / serving	1 to 2 servings 3 to 4 servings	High (10) High (10)	1 to 2 2 to 3
	Tip: Cover saucy main dishes with plastic wrap. Cover other main dishes and meats with wax paper. Do not cover rare or medium rare meats.			

Item	Amount	Power Level	Approx. Time, Minutes
Sandwiches Moist filling			
sloppy joe, barbecue, ham salad, etc. in bun	1 to 2 servings	Medium High (7)	1 to 2
1/3 cup / serving	3 to 4 servings	Medium High (7)	2 to 3
Thick meat-cheese filling with firm bread	1 to 2 servings	Medium High (7)	1 to 2
	3 to 4 servings	Medium High (7)	2 to 3
Soup			
Water based 1 cup / serving	1 to 2 servings	High (10)	1 to 2
	3 to 4 servings	High (10)	3 to 5
	1 10-oz. can reconstituted	High (10)	3 to 4
Milk based 1 cup / serving	1 to 2 servings	Medium High (7)	2 to 4
	3 to 4 servings	Medium High (7)	4 to 5
	1 10-oz. can reconstituted	Medium High (7)	5 to 6
Tip: Use paper towel or napkin to cover sandwiches. Cover soups with wax paper or plastic wrap.			
Vegetables Small pieces			
peas, beans, corn, etc.	1 to 2 servings	High (10)	1 to 2
½ cup / serving	3 to 4 servings	High (10)	2 to 3
	1 16-oz. can	High (10)	2 to 4
Large pieces or whole	1 to 2 servings	High (10)	1 to 2
asparagus spears, corn on the cob, etc.	3 to 4 servings	High (10)	3 to 4
	1 16-oz. can	High (10)	4
Mashed potatoes, squash, pumpkin, etc.	1 to 2 servings	High (10)	1 to 2
½ cup / serving	3 to 4 servings	High (10)	2 to 4
Tip: Cover vegetables for most even heating.			
Sauces Dessert: chocolate or butterscotch	½ cup	High (10)	1
	1 cup	High (10)	2 to 3
Meat or main dish, chunky type	½ cup	High (10)	1
giblet gravy, spaghetti sauce, etc.	1 cup	High (10)	2 to 3
	1 16-oz. can	High (10)	3 to 4
Creamy type	½ cup	High (10)	1
	1 cup	High (10)	2 to 2½
Tip: Cover food to prevent spatter.			
Bakery Foods Cake, coffee cake, doughnuts, sweet rolls, nut or fruit bread	1 piece	Low (3)	½ to 1
	2 pieces	Low (3)	1 to 1½
	9-inch cake or 12 rolls or doughnuts	Low (3)	2 to 4
Dinner rolls, muffins	1	Medium (5)	¼ to ½
	2 to 4	Medium (5)	½ to 1
	6 to 8	Medium (5)	1 to 2
Pie fruit, nut or custard	1 slice	High (10)	½ to 1
1/8 of 9-inch pie = 1 slice	2 slices	High (10)	1 to 1½
(use minimum time for custard)	9-inch pie	Medium High (7)	4 to 6
Griddle Foods Pancakes, French toast or waffles			
Plain, no topping	2 to 3 pieces	High (10)	½ to 1
With syrup & butter	2 or 3 pieces	High (10)	1 to 2
With 2 sausage patties (cooked)	2 or 3 pieces	High (10)	1 to 2
Beverages Coffee, tea, cider, other water based	1 to 2 cups	High (10)	1 to 3
	3 to 4 cups	High (10)	4 to 6
Cocoa, other milk based	1 to 2 cups	Medium High (7)	3 to 5
	3 to 4 cups	Medium High (7)	5 to 6

Convection Baking Chart

1. Always use metal accessory rack when convection baking. (See Use & Care Book.)
2. Aluminum pans conduct heat quickly. For most convection baking, light shiny finishes give best results because they prevent overbrowning in the time it takes to cook the center areas. Pans with dull (satin-finish) bottoms are recommended for cake pans and pie pans for best bottom browning.
3. Dark or non-shiny finishes, glass and pyroceram absorb heat which may result in dry, crisp crusts.
4. Preheating the oven is recommended when baking foods by convection.
5. To prevent uneven heating and save energy, open the oven door to check food as little as possible.

FOOD		Oven Temp.	Time, Min.	Comments
Breads	Biscuits	450°	11 to 13	Canned refrigerated biscuits take 2 to 4 minutes less time.
	Corn Bread	400°	15 to 20	
	Muffins	375°	15 to 20	Remove from pans immediately and cool slightly on wire rack.
	Popovers	350°	30 to 40	Prick each popover with a fork after removing from oven to allow steam to escape.
	Nut Bread or Fruit Bread	350°	55 to 65	Interiors will be moist and tender.
	Yeast Bread	375°	18 to 25	
	Plain or Sweet Rolls	350°	13 to 16	Lightly grease baking sheet.
Cakes	Angel Food	350°	40 to 50	Invert and cool in pan.
	Cheesecake	350°	60 to 65	After cooking, turn oven off and let cheesecake stand in oven 30 minutes with door ajar.
	Coffee Cake	350°	25 to 30	
	Cup Cakes	350°	15 to 20	
	Fruit Cake (loaf)	300°	80 to 90	Interior will be moist and tender.
	Gingerbread	350°	35 to 40	
	Butter Cakes, Cake Mixes (2 layers)	350°	30 to 40	Use 2 shelves. Top layer may bake in less time.
	Fluted Tube Cake	350°	40 to 50	Grease and flour pan.
	Pound Cake	350°	60 to 70	Cool in pan 10 minutes before inverting on wire rack.
Cookies	Bar	350°	35 to 45	Use same time for bar cookies from a mix.
	Drop or Sliced	375°	11 to 16	Use same time for sliced cookies from a mix.

Convection Baking Chart *continued*

FOOD		Oven Temp.	Time, Min.	Comments
Fruits, Other Desserts	Baked Apples or Pears	350°	30 to 40	Bake in utensil with shallow sides.
	Bread Pudding	300°	35 to 40	Pudding is done when knife inserted near center comes out clean.
	Cream Puffs	400°	30 to 35	Puncture puffs twice with toothpick to release steam after 25 minutes of baking time.
	Custard (individual)	350°	45 to 50	Set cups in baking dish. Pour boiling water around cups to a depth of 1 inch.
	Meringue Shells	300°	30 to 35	When done, turn oven off and let shells stand in oven 1 hour to dry.
Pies, Pastries	Frozen	375°	40 to 45	Follow procedure on package.
	Meringue-topped	325°	13 to 16	
	Two-crust	400°	50 to 55	
	Quiche	350°	30 to 35	Let stand 5 minutes before cutting.
	Pastry Shell	400°	10 to 14	Prick pastry with fork to prevent shrinkage.
Casseroles	Meat, chicken, seafood combinations	350°	20 to 40	Cook times vary with casserole size and ingredients.
	Pasta	350°	25 to 45	Cook times vary with casserole size and ingredients.
	Potatoes, scalloped	350°	55 to 60	Let stand 5 minutes before serving.
	Vegetable	350°	25 to 35	Cook times vary with casserole size and ingredients.
Convenience Foods	Frozen Bread Dough	350°	30 to 35	
	Frozen Dinners	350°	20 to 25	Follow package directions.
	Frozen Entrees	350°	50 to 60	Follow package directions.
	Frozen Pizza Rolls, Egg Rolls	400°	8 to 10	Follow package directions.
	Pizza	425°	15 to 25	
	Slice and Bake Cookies	375°	13 to 15	Let stand a few minutes before removing from pan to cool.
Main Dishes	Meat Loaf	325°	55 to 60	
	Oven-baked Stew	325°	80 to 90	Brown meat before combining with liquid and vegetables.
	Swiss Steak	350°	60 to 70	
	Stuffed Peppers	350°	40 to 45	Use green, red or yellow peppers.
Vegetables	Acorn Squash Halves	375°	55 to 60	Pierce skin in several places. Add ¼ cup water to dish. Turn squash halves cut side up after 30 minutes of cook time and cover.
	Baked Potatoes	425°	50 to 60	Prick skins with a fork before baking. Use 2 shelves, if desired.
	Twice-Baked Potatoes	400°	25 to 30	

Meat Roasting Chart for Convection Cooking

MEATS		Minutes / Lb..	Oven Temp.	Internal Temp
Beef	Rib (3 to 5 lbs.)			
	Rare	27 to 32	325°	140°
	Medium	32 to 37	325°	160°
	Well	37 to 42	325°	170°
	Boneless Rib, Top Sirloin			
	Rare	33 to 38	325°	140°
	Medium	38 to 43	325°	160°
	Well	43 to 48	325°	170°
	Beef Tenderloin			
	Rare	18 to 21	325°	140°
	Medium	21 to 25	325°	160°
	Pot Roast (2½ to 3 lbs.)			
	Chuck, Rump	50 to 55	325°	170°
Ham	Canned (3-lb. fully cooked)	25 to 28	325°	140°
	Butt (5-lb. fully cooked)	25 to 28	325°	140°
	Shank (5-lb. fully cooked)	22 to 25	325°	140°
Lamb	Bone-in (3 to 5 lbs.)			
	Medium	26 to 31	325°	160°
	Well	31 to 36	325°	170°
	Boneless (3 to 5 lbs.)			
	Medium	30 to 35	325°	160°
	Well	34 to 39	325°	170°
Pork	Bone-in (3 to 5 lbs.)	31 to 35	325°	170°
	Boneless (3 to 5 lbs.)	37 to 41	325°	170°
	Pork Chops (½ to 1-inch thick)			
	2 chops	35 to 40 total	325°	170°
	4 chops	40 to 45 total	325°	170°
	6 chops	45 to 50 total	325°	170°
Poultry	Whole Chicken (2½ to 3½ lbs.)	25 to 30 total	375°	180° to 185°
	Chicken Pieces (2½ to 3½ lbs.)	35 to 45 total	350°	180° to 185°
	Cornish Hens			
	Unstuffed (1 to 1½ lbs.)	50 to 55 total	375°	180° to 185°
	Stuffed (1 to 1½ lbs.)	60 to 65 total	375°	180° to 185°
	Duckling (4 to 5 lbs.)	24 to 26	375°	180° to 185°
	Turkey Breast (4 to 6 lbs.)	26 to 30	325°	170°
Seafood	Fish, whole (3 to 5 lbs.)	30 to 40 total	400°	
	Lobster Tails (6 to 8-oz. each)	20 to 25 total	350°	

Meat Roasting Chart for Combination Cooking

MEATS		Combination Temperature	Minutes / Lb.	Temperature or Probe Setting
Beef	Rib (3 to 5 lbs.)			
	Rare	300°	14 to 17	140°
	Medium	300°	17 to 20	160°
	Well	300°	20 to 23	170°
	Boneless Rib, Top Sirloin			
	Rare	300°	12 to 15	140°
	Medium	300°	15 to 18	160°
	Well	300°	18 to 21	170°
	Beef Tenderloin			
	Rare	300°	17 to 20	140°
	Medium	300°	20 to 23	160°
	Chuck, Rump or Pot Roast (2½ to 3 lbs.) (Use cooking bag for best results.)	275°	1½ to 2 hours total	170°
	Turn over after half of cooking time.			
Ham	Canned (3-lb. fully cooked)	300°	13 to 16	140°
	Butt (5-lb. fully cooked)	300°	13 to 16	140°
	Shank (5-lb. fully cooked)	300°	13 to 16	140°
	Turn over after half of cooking time.			
Lamb	Bone-in (3 to 5 lbs.)			
	Medium	300°	12 to 17	140°
	Well	300°	17 to 22	160°
	Boneless (3 to 5 lbs.)			
	Medium	300°	13 to 18	140°
	Well	300°	18 to 23	160°
	Turn over after half of cooking time.			
Pork	Bone-in (3 to 5 lbs.)	300°	16 to 19	170°
	Boneless (3 to 5 lbs.)	300°	17 to 20	170°
	Pork Chops (¾ to 1-inch thick)			
	2 chops	350°	29 to 34 total	
	4 chops	350°	35 to 40 total	
	6 chops	350°	41 to 46 total	
	Turn over after half of cooking time.			
Poultry	Whole Chicken (2½ to 3½ lbs.)	375°	40 to 50 total	180° to 185°
	Chicken Pieces (2½ to 3½ lbs.)	375°	38 to 43 total	180° to 185°
	Cornish Hens			
	Unstuffed	375°	65 to 75 total	180° to 185°
	Stuffed	375°	75 to 80 total	180° to 185°
	Duckling	375°	60 to 70 total	180° to 185°
	Turkey Breast (4 to 6 lbs.) Turn breast side up after half of cooking time.	300°	13 to 17	170°
Seafood	Fish 1-lb. fillets	350°	7 to 10 total	
	Lobster Tails (6 to 8-oz. each)	350°	13 to 18 total	
	Shrimp (1 to 2 lbs.)	350°	10 to 13 total	
	Scallops (1 to 2 lbs.)	350°	10 to 13 total	

Index

Index

Index

CREDITS:
Brigid Lally Bowles
Manager, Consumer Information
Testing Laboratory
GE Appliances

Marilyn Rollins, Home Economist

Design, Production, Photography
and Food Styling:
OTT Communications, Inc.
Louisville, Kentucky